Anarchy Explained to My Father

ANARCHY
EXPLAINED TO MY FATHER
FRANCIS DUPUIS-DÉRI & THOMAS DÉRI

Translated from the French by JOHN GILMORE

New Star Books / Vancouver / 2017

NEW STAR BOOKS LTD.

107–3477 Commercial Street, Vancouver, BC V5N 4E8   CANADA
1574 Gulf Road, No. 1517, Point Roberts, WA 98281   USA
www.NewStarBooks.com   info@NewStarBooks.com

Originally published in French as *L'anarchie expliquée à mon père* by
Lux Éditeur (2014).

The publisher acknowledges the financial support of the Canada
Council for the Arts and the British Columbia Arts Council.

We acknowledge the financial support of the government of Canada
through the National Translation Program for Book Publishing, an
initiative of the *Roadmap for Canada's Official Languages 2013–2018:
Education, Immigration, Communities*, for our translation activities.

Cataloguing information for this book is available from
Library and Archives Canada, www.collectionscanada.gc.ca.

Cover design by Oliver McPartlin / mcpartlin.ca
Cover photo by Vita Vilcina / Unsplash.com
Printed on 100% post-consumer recycled paper
Printed and bound in Canada by Imprimerie Gauvin
First printing, October 2017

For Catherine, Colette, Marie-Eve, and Mélissa

TRANSLATOR'S NOTE: This translation incorporates changes by the authors to the original 2014 French edition.

I am grateful to the Canada Council for the Arts for funding this translation, to Collège international des traducteurs littéraires, in Arles, France, for a residency to work on it, and to Martin Duckworth and Audrey Schirmer for their generous hospitality.

Contents

THOMAS DÉRI: Almost a thousand years ago the French philosopher Bernard de Chartres said, "We are dwarfs, standing on the shoulders of giants." He meant that every generation builds on the achievements of previous generations. Now that I'm old and can look back at all the changes and discoveries that have taken place over the past fifty years, I wonder if the real giants today aren't the younger generations. Everything is changing so fast that even simple words change their meanings, and new concepts force us to question many things we've taken for granted.

There was a time, in the Western world, when we used to respect our elders. We believed that with age came experience and wisdom. Now we label them "senior citizens" and "the elderly," and put them in special residences, out of the way.

When I was a child, I was always pestering my parents to explain the world to me. "Why, why?" I kept asking. Sometimes they knew the answer. Other times, exasperated, they just said, "Because!" Now that I'm retired (from work, though not from life), I have ample time to reflect on the meaning of things, and consider why people behave the way they do.

One thing I've noticed: when I'm discussing things with younger people, we often use the same words, but with different meanings. Simple words like *love*, *family*, *man*, *woman*, and *education* have new meanings now. Adjectives like *young*, *old*, *masculine*, and *feminine* no longer qualify nouns in the same way. Other words and expressions have become politically incorrect, replaced by circumlocutions or metaphors devoid of substance, like the word *deaf* replaced by *hard of hearing*, or *student* replaced by *learner*.

For a long time I puzzled over the meaning of *democracy*, a key word that everyone lays claim to. Eventually I realized there are as many democracies as there are self-proclaimed democrats, and I was wasting my time trying to pin down a word used by chameleons everywhere.

I'm fortunate to have a daughter and a son who don't consider me an old fogey. We can discuss things without descending into intergenerational conflict. My daughter is a senior officer in the Canadian military and intensely interested in questions of leadership. My son teaches political science at a university and wrote a doctoral dissertation on democracy. I observed his thesis defence, four days before 9/11 — that day when the world changed and the word *democracy* suddenly took on several new meanings. And then *terrorism* became the new key word.

But life went on ... The news is arriving faster and faster. Everyone is flying off in different directions these days, and we no longer seem capable of making thought-ful connections between events, of seeing cause and effect. And so I've started wondering whether the key word in these early years of the twenty-first century shouldn't be *anarchy*.

Luckily, my son teaches a seminar called "Theories and Practices of Anarchism," which introduces students to the political and philosophical questions posed by anarchism. So, I turn to you now, Francis, and invite you to explain anarchy to me. Think of me, if you want, as representative of the generation molded by the experience of the Second World War. But I'm warning you right at the start—I won't accept "because" for an answer!

Democracy and Anarchism

FRANCIS DUPUIS-DÉRI: It's interesting: you used the word *democracy* before mentioning *anarchy*. For a long time the two words were almost synonymous, especially in the United States and France. Until the mid-nineteenth century, *democracy* referred to a political system in ancient Athens, where power was exercised by a popular assembly in which all citizens could participate in decisions affecting their common affairs. But this concept of democracy had a pejorative taint in the West. The problem with Athenian democracy, according to its detractors, was not just that women, slaves, and foreigners didn't have the right to enter the agora and participate in debates. The problem went much deeper: it was an irrational and chaotic system of government, and inherently violent. Why? Because it was a system controlled by the majority, and the poor are always in the majority. So, critics argued, Athenian-style democracy would give the poor power, which they would use to attack the rich and destroy private property. Hence the idea of chaos and violence; hence the idea that democracy is anarchy, because the poor would never respect legitimate authority or the established hierarchical social order. To the elite, the very idea of democracy was scandalous.

The eighteenth century gave us the American War of Independence (1775–1783) and the French Revolution (1789). But almost no one at that time used the word *democracy* in a positive sense. The people we think of as the founding fathers of "modern democracy" in the United States and France were openly anti-democratic. They used the word *democracy* as a bogeyman in their speeches and writings; to call someone a *democrat* was an insult. They wanted to create a republic that was opposed to the monarchy and the aristocracy, but also to democracy, understood as a system in which the people, the majority of them poor, govern themselves without leaders. The republican elite considered this idea a political aberration and a moral threat. They insisted that the people needed enlightened leaders who were morally and intellectually superior to the ordinary people. In saying that, they were simply legitimizing their own power, for in their view power naturally resided in the upper class. Hence an observer remarked in 1790 that the French Revolution had simply replaced the "hereditary aristocracy" with an "elected aristocracy." In other words, the newly elected representatives in France's National Assembly had become the new elite, the new aristocracy.

That new elite believed that "the people" was a mass of selfish and irrational individuals who had no clear vision for society and were incapable of understanding the idea of "the common good." That explains why, when you delve into eighteenth-century archives, you find so many anti-democratic statements. For example, John Adams, one of the most important leaders of the American independence movement and the second president of the United States, said, "I was always for a free republic, not a democracy, which is ... arbitrary, tyrannical, bloody, cruel, and intolerable." Can you imagine an American president saying that today?

Many ordinary people are convinced they need leaders to guide them. They get swept up in admiration for their leaders. They venerate them, even sacrifice their lives in their name. In the United States and France, the first people to call themselves *democrats* and lay claim to the word *democracy* were egalitarians who dreamt of doing away with distinctions between rich and poor, between the governed and those who govern. During the French Revolution, for example, Sylvain Maréchal put forth such radical ideas in his *Manifesto of the Equals:* "Disappear at least, revolting distinctions between rich and poor, great and small, masters and servants, *rulers* and *ruled*. Let there no longer be any difference between people except those of age and sex."

THOMAS: So when did we start using the word *democracy* in a positive sense, to describe our political systems?

FRANCIS: Around 1840, the political elite in the United States and France began championing the idea of democracy. They appropriated the word *democracy* when they realized it could win them votes. By associating themselves with the word, the elite gave the impression that they were listening to the people and serving the people's interests. This coincided with the creation of new states in the western USA, where smallholders were more likely to vote for politicians who pretended to identity with the common folk. Andrew Jackson, elected in 1828, was the first US president to describe himself as a democrat. Newspapers who supported him called him the defender of "democracy and the people against a corrupt aristocracy." In France, during the 1848 elections that followed the February Revolution, moderate and conservative republicans appropriated the words *democracy* and *democrat* from the socialists, hoping to give the impression that they cared about the people. Within a few short years, *democracy* had been appropriated by all camps, even the monarchists! In Canada, which is still a constitutional monarchy, the political elites began identifying themselves with the word *democracy* during the First World War, as a way of bolstering support for the war effort. The population was told that their sacrifice was for the common good and to protect people's freedom.

THOMAS: So, if I'm understanding you correctly, what was originally called democracy is really anarchy, and what we call anarchy is really a contemporary form of democracy—if such a thing in fact exists.

FRANCIS: Yes, if by democracy you mean direct democracy, where everyone can gather at the agora, participate in the debate, and collectively make decisions about things affecting their common interests. The word anarchy has now replaced democracy as the new bogeyman; it's the word used to scare the public and denounce popular, grassroots initiatives.

THOMAS: Perhaps we should also clarify that the word democracy predates the very idea of "the state." Democracy entered the French language around 1370; the idea of the state didn't appear until around 1500. The state originally meant "a group of people submitting to the same authority," though the meaning quickly shifted to "the sovereign authority exercised over a people and a territory." The word anarchy, in its classical, technical sense, meant "a political state in which the enfranchised can play a role in government." So anarchists can participate in government!

FRANCIS: Yes, if we understand the word *government* to mean the body that decides common affairs. A government can be a popular assembly where everybody is allowed to participate. The government and the state are not necessarily the same thing. As you point out, the vocabulary we have inherited from ancient Greece can be misleading, because in ancient Greece there was no state as we understand it today. There were only cities (Athens, Sparta, etc.), which sometimes built empires. In the Middle Ages there were kingdoms, but they were nothing like states, either. There were, however, governments—monarchical governments, in which the king imposed his will on his kingdom, or even feudal governments, since all nobles held some power, depending on their rank.

At the dawn of modernity, around the beginning of the sixteenth century, the term "feudal anarchy" was used to describe the political situation during the preceding Middle Ages, when the king (the monarch) had only a little control over the nobles (the aristocrats), who ran their domains as they pleased and waged war against each other. That created, some felt, a situation of "anarchy."

THOMAS: If, as you say, the word *anarchy* has replaced *democracy* as the bogeyman, to scare the public and demonize grassroots initiatives, this substitution couldn't have happened until the idea of the state was born.

FRANCIS: Indeed. The concept of the state arose in the West at the dawn of modernity, at the same time as notions of political systems and institutions were taking shape. This development happened very slowly. It wasn't until the state began imposing a complex system of control over a population and territory, in the mid-nineteenth century, that people started calling themselves *anarchists*. They were opposed to both the state and to other forms of authority, such as the church and capitalism. They argued that the word *democracy* was a trap for the people, and so were elections. The elite had appropriated the word *democracy* for its own benefit, so these anti-establishment people had to find a new name. And that's how the word *anarchist* came into being.

In 1848 a French writer and editor named Anselme Bellegarrigue published a manifesto called *Au fait! Au fait! Interprétation de l'idée démocratique* (Get to the point! To the point! An interpretation of the idea of democracy). Bellegarrigue was one of the first to call himself an anarchist. In a later manifesto he said that anarchy is "the condition of a people who, wanting to govern themselves, lack a government precisely because they don't want one." In another work he described anarchy as,

> from the vantage point of absolute or democratic truth, nothing less than the true expression of social order. . . .
>
> Who says anarchy, says negation of government;
>
> Who says negation of government says affirmation of the people;
>
> Who says affirmation of the people, says individual liberty;
>
> Who says individual liberty, says sovereignty of each;
>
> Who says sovereignty of each, says equality;
>
> Who says equality, says solidarity or fraternity;
>
> Who says fraternity, says social order. . . .
>
> Yes, anarchy is order.

Essentially, the elites argued that the majority (i.e., the poor) weren't capable of governing themselves without unleashing chaos, or anarchy. The early anarchists countered that freedom, equality, solidarity, and even social order would never be achieved until the distinction disappeared between the governed and those who govern, and everyone could participate equally in collective decision-making. As long as there were leaders and subordinates, they argued, there would be tensions and social conflicts, and there could never be true freedom and equality.

THOMAS: I always knew that words evolve over time, but I never imagined that words could come to mean the exact opposite of their initial meaning. What are the implications of this? When we read a text do we have to stop and ascertain the date of every word and concept in order to understand the meaning?

FRANCIS: For the history of the word *anarchy*, at least in French, a good place to start is a scholarly work by Marc Deleplace called *L'anarchie de Mably à Proudhon: 1750–1850* (Anarchy from Mably to Proudhon: 1750–1850). It reveals that while anarchy was often talked about during the French Revolution, anarchists themselves had not yet mapped out a distinct political terrain. Anarchists were regarded as "the other," the enemy, the one you fought against because you were on the side of "the good." It wasn't until around 1840 that revolutionaries started calling themselves anarchists and championing anarchy. Among them was the Russian revolutionary Mikhail Bakunin, who published a text in German, in the journal *Deutschen Jahrbüchern*, in which he aligned himself with anarchy. For Bakunin, that meant to be against the state and religion.

THOMAS: What about the word *libertarian*, meaning someone who doesn't recognize any limitations on individual freedom, either social or political. Is a libertarian basically the same as an anarchist?

FRANCIS: Yes. In fact, it was a French anarchist, Joseph Déjacque, who first used the word *libertaire* (libertarian) to describe a political position, in the mid-nineteenth century. Since then, the word *libertarian* is sometimes used instead of *anarchist* because it implies a more positive vision. *Anarchist* has negative connotations, and has often been used pejoratively. But the two words basically mean the same.*

In practice, the words *democracy* (in its original sense) and *anarchy* are also basically the same: the community makes decisions collectively, in an assembly or a committee, and all members of the community can—in principle—participate directly in the deliberations. Where they differ is that in democracy the decision is made by the majority, which can leave the minority feeling dominated. But in anarchy you seek consensus, meaning a decision that everyone can agree with, or at least that no one is opposed to. In both systems, the people don't elect leaders to govern them.

By the way, anarchists were urging people to abstain from elections as far back as the nineteenth century. The early anarchists despised this "silly and childish right to choose our masters," as Bellegarrigue put it. This was at a time when men, many of them impoverished, were demanding the right to vote in several countries. Even when they won the right, women and children were

---

* In the United States in particular, the English word *libertarian* is often used to describe a right-wing philosophy of radical individualism which rests on the belief that individual freedom can only flourish within free market capitalism. Throughout this translation I use *libertarian* in its original, leftist sense, as more or less synonymous with *anarchist*. —Trans.

denied it. Elections are always a trap because the people we choose to govern in our name hold power and inevitably impose their will on us. If aristocracy is government by a small minority, then the electoral system produces an elected aristocracy. That may be better than a hereditary aristocracy, but it's still an aristocracy and certainly not a democracy, if words still mean anything.

THOMAS: I understand why anarchists abstain from voting: because they don't want to participate in a system that just substitutes one authority for another. Octave Mirbeau put it well, in 1888:

> There's something that astounds me enormously. In fact, I'd even say that it stupefies me, and that's that at this scientific moment when I'm writing, after countless experiences, after daily scandals, there can still exist . . . one single voter — that irrational, inorganic, hallucinatory animal — who consents to put a halt to his affairs, his dreams, and his pleasures in order to vote in favour of someone or something.

But I guess there will always be enough people to go out and vote, believing that democracy is synonymous with "the right to vote." In a wonderful novel called *Seeing*, José Saramago describes the electoral panic that follows when 83 percent of the voters leave their ballots blank. Chaos erupts; the government sees it as a conspiracy and declares a state of siege. Perhaps that's the way anarchists can gum up the electoral system!

FRANCIS: Did you know that Saramago once called himself a "libertarian communist"? Nowadays, voting is extolled as a sacred act, and not voting is judged a sin. There's something very strange about this public condemnation of abstention. Voter turnout has never affected the ability of the state to function. In the nineteenth century, Great Britain was the most powerful nation in the liberal world, but only 15 percent of adult males had the right to vote. Nowadays, even if the politicians that govern us win only 30 percent of the popular vote, the state carries on functioning: it continues to wage wars, sign treaties, impose taxes, and pay civil servants to manage public works and administer the courts, schools, and prisons. I think what makes abstention so offensive in the eyes of those who vote is that it undermines the credibility of an act to which society attributes so much importance.

Anarchists sometimes campaign for abstention and dream of the day when abstainers will be the majority. It's absurd: in Quebec, the law requires those who campaign for abstention to register with the chief electoral officer and file accounts of their expenses, which are strictly limited by law. Obviously, anarchists don't bother.

What is Anarchy?

THOMAS: Let's return to my first question, "What is anarchy?" Let's start with the dictionary definitions. I have a 1972 edition of the Larousse dictionary, which defines *anarchy* as follows: "(from the Greek *anarkhia*, absence of a ruler). Political and social system in which the individual is free of all government tutelage. State in which a people, virtually and in fact, no longer have a government. By extension: disorder, confusion: an anarchic enterprise or rule, anarchy of spirit." Note that it uses the words *ruler* and *tutelage*. Now compare that with the 2008 edition of the same dictionary: "(Greek, *anarkhia*, absence of leader). 1. Anarchism. 2. A state of unrest and disorder due to the suppression of political authority and lack of laws. 3. State of general confusion: 'Anarchy reigns in this department.'" The 2008 Larousse also defines *anarchism* as "the political doctrine that advocates the suppression of the State and of all social constraints on the individual." So, in thirty-odd years, the definition has evolved from the absence of government to the absence of all social constraints!

Another dictionary I found, from 1992, defines *anarchy* as "a state of disorder caused by the absence of political authority" and *anarchism* as "a doctrine that rejects all authority."

So let me ask you this: Is there any real distinction to be made among the words *anarchy*, *anarchism*, and *anarchist*? Or are the three inseparable? When we speak of one are we necessarily speaking of the other two?

What really interests me are the facts on the ground and the people involved, the men and women activists. I'm less interested in theory, though I accept that we can't really talk about one without the other, because the activists and theoreticians have inspired one other, and the theoreticians have themselves often been activists. All the big names—Proudhon, Bellegarrigue, Bakunin, Thoreau, Reclus, Kropotkin, Malatesta, Louise Michel, Voltairine de Cleyre, Emma Goldman—they were all either imprisoned, deported, or exiled. So, clear something up for me right away: are anarchy and anarchism the same thing?

FRANCIS: Good question! In fact, anarchy and anarchism are not exactly the same. *Anarchism* generally refers to the philosophy or ideology of anarchists; in other words, their theories and concepts, their arguments in favour of anarchy. In a nutshell, anarchism is both a negative idea, a critique, and a positive idea, a political program. In its critical sense, anarchism is the negation of all forms of domination, authority, hierarchy, and inequality. In its positive sense, anarchism proposes that we organize social relations and human relationships in a way that makes true freedom, equality, and solidarity possible. To achieve that, we need autonomy, self-management, anarchist communism (i.e., communism without a state or governing party), and mutual aid. Anarchism can also refer to the anarchist movement, with its activists, organizations, and committees, its campaigns and demonstrations—and sometimes its insurrections and rebellions.

By *anarchy* we mean the lived experience of a social practice without leaders or hierarchy. Anarchy's detractors see that as chaos, whereas anarchy's supporters talk more in terms of individual and collective freedom, equality, and mutual aid. The usual way it's expressed is "order without power," meaning community-based, collective organization without power, authority, or coercion, and without rules or punishments. How does such a community function, in practice? By its members discussing the things that affect them, in both formal and informal agoras. The deliberations can take different forms, including lengthy debates, meetings of all members, and committees.

If I had to chose between theory and practice, i.e., between anarchism and anarchy, I'd say practice is more important. Anarchism as a political philosophy or ideology is rooted in the actual social and political experience of anarchy. Peter Kropotkin, a Russian anarchist who died in 1921, said in his book *Modern Science and Anarchism*: "As Socialism in general, Anarchism was born *among the people*; and it will continue to be full of life and creative power only as long as it remains a thing of the people." Which is to say that it's the people who developed the ideas of anarchism, in their speeches and directly in their experiences and their various organizations. Kropotkin is cautioning us that anarchism is not a theory developed by scholars.

Obviously, academics can teach courses on anarchism (as I do) and publish scholarly articles about anarchism (as I do). This is happening more and more, especially in the English-speaking academic world. There are conferences on anarchism, and specialized publications on the subject. When the alter-globalization movement got going around the year 2000, there were a lot of anarchists and people sympathetic to anarchy involved in the movement, and with that came a surge in the popularity of anarchism at universities. More and more anarchists have found positions in departments of anthropology, geography, philosophy, sociology, and political science. There's even talk of anarchism reaching a watershed moment, especially in English-speaking universities.

But let's face it: most academics publish their ideas in specialist journals and write in an abstract language that the general public and activists have a hard time relating to. I'm thinking, for example, of the debate about post-anarchism versus classic anarchism or neo-anarchism. In a nutshell, post-anarchism revives the theories and concepts of popular, post-structural intellectuals such as Gilles Deleuze, Michel Foucault, and Jean-François Lyotard. Post-anarchism offers a theoretical framework which its proponents claim is better suited to contemporary reality: it sees power as diffuse rather than concentrated at the top, and it favours individual initiatives and tactical struggles. Post-anarchism claims to have emancipated itself from classical anarchism; the latter is said to be dogmatic and naive in its affirmation that human beings are perfectible, history is progressive, science is inherently valuable, and the global revolution is just within reach. English-speaking academics have been debating this since the 1990s. There are monographs, essay collections, and special issues of academic journals devoted to the subject. In France, the intellectual Michel Onfray published a book called *Le post-anarchisme expliqué à ma grand-mère* (Post-anarchism explained to my grandmother) in which he lays out the basic ideas of post-anarchism, though he neglects to mention those who have been reflecting on the subject for years.

All this is interesting from an intellectual and theoretical point of view, but it has almost nothing to do with the actual political experiences of most anarchists. Post-anarchist theoreticians cite Deleuze and Foucault, but rarely the writings or experiences of real activists. The impression post-anarchist theoreticians give of classic anarchism is false, a caricature that serves no other purpose than to make classic anarchism look old-fashioned and ridiculous, the better to claim that post-anarchism is a new and improved formula. And yet some activists have developed ideas similar to those of the famous intellectuals, about power for example. What's more, the activists dare to hope for a revolution, and engage in individual actions and tactical struggles.

We should never lose sight of the fact that as anarchism becomes increasingly popular in the university and the arts, it's often the elites in those circles whose interests are served by these debates. I myself write scholarly articles about pure political philosophy, both because I enjoy doing so and because it's part of my job as an academic. But I regularly remind myself that my scholarly articles have no importance outside my milieu, least of all for anarchists who are active in social protest movements.

Let's never forget that the university is a hierarchical institution. It's built on inequality. It encourages social distinctions by awarding degrees. Essentially, the university produces tomorrow's elite—doctors, engineers, lawyers, administrators, middle and upper managers, and specialists in various fields.

The university where I teach, Université du Québec à Montréal, is one of the most dynamic in Canada in terms of developing original, critical thought. (It's also the nerve centre of a gutsy Quebec student movement). And yet 30 percent of the students are in management studies, which means ten thousand young people dreaming of becoming bosses, administrators, or consultants for government or private industry. Even departments such as political science, social work, and psychology, which you'd expect to be open to new ideas, tend to be quite conservative, effectively preparing students to exercise social control. It should come as no surprise that some anarchists believe the university is beyond reform and should simply be destroyed, to make way for new ways of educating and training people.

So I wouldn't put too much hope in the anarchism espoused by academics and ivory tower intellectuals. Many people in France consider Michel Onfray a living giant of anarchism. But he's content to preach anarchism from prestigious podiums, while scorning activists themselves. Michael Paraire reproached him for this in a scathing pamphlet called *Michel Onfray, une imposture intellectuelle* (Michel Onfray, an intellectual imposter). Onfray takes offence at such criticism. Yet it's entirely consistent for anarchists to take aim at academics (myself included) who build careers and make names for ourselves in the media by claiming to be experts on anarchism. There's more to anarchism than declaring your values and flaunting your knowledge. Anarchism demands an ethical choice, to reject the privileged status that an elitist system bestows on us, and the benefits that come with it. In anarchy, there should be no more distinctions between masters and disciples, between intellectuals and manual labourers. Those (like me) who claim to be sympathetic to anarchism and anarchists while speaking from prestigious podiums should be prepared for harsh criticism because, seen from an anarchist perspective, the choice we have made is full of contradictions.

Certainly, public personalities like Michel Onfray in France and Noam Chomsky in the United States can inspire others to explore anarchism, and even to "become" anarchists. (By the way, Chomsky is much less arrogant than Onfray, and much more sympathetic to anarchism.) Personally, I discovered anarchism when I was fifteen or sixteen through the music of Bérurier Noir and books such as Daniel Guérin's *Anarchism: From Theory to Practice* and *No Gods, No Masters*. But it was only by becoming active in groups that function in an anarchist manner, groups that make decisions collectively through consensus, that I came to truly understood what anarchy is and what it's capable of achieving in the real world.

THOMAS: I understand the distinction you're making between anarchism the theory and anarchy the practice. But if most theoreticians are also "practitioners" then anarchists aren't really taking their cue from a theory or a philosophy, are they? They're just rebelling against a state of affairs that they consider harmful, one that creates inequalities and injustices in society.

FRANCIS: Let's go even further: unlike other ideologies, such as Marxism, anarchy doesn't go looking for absolute truths in the books of the forefathers. Because if you revere the great names of the past in that way, then you're perpetuating a system of domination and inequality. With Marxism, which takes its very name from Karl Marx, people often believe they have to conform to his thinking and adhere to a school of thought created by one of his followers, such as Maoism, Leninism, Trotskyism, or Guevarism. In contrast, here's how an independent collective of Bolivian feminist activists called Mujeres Creando (Creative women) describe their anarchist affinities: "We are not anarchists by [way of] Bakunin or the

CNT [National Confederation of Labour], but rather by [way of] our grandmothers, and that's a beautiful school of anarchism." In other words, the most important thing is concrete experience, action, and the implementation of ideas.

That doesn't mean anarchists aren't interested in writings and theories. Since the nineteenth century, anarchists have started newspapers, popular libraries, and documentation centres, and run popular workshops to develop and disseminate their ideas. But books should be sources of inspiration, not sacred texts. They should stimulate reflection rather than blind faith. That's how you have to understand references to the "great authors" of anarchism, while also remembering that most of them were experienced activists.

That's also true for the great names of Marxism, like Lenin, Mao, and Castro: they were both influential authors and hardened militants, and often suffered severe repression. But anarchists have never tried to take power in the name of the proletariat, whereas Lenin, Mao, and Castro did. And once they took power, their books became sacred texts, and reading them became obligatory.

You asked me before for examples of real anarchists. Here are a few whose theoretical writings were directly shaped by their experience. Mikhail Bakunin participated in several militant groups, including the First International, until he was forced out by Karl Marx and his faction. Bakunin also took part in several uprisings, which landed him in prison.

Louise Michel was a key figure in the Paris Commune. When she was deported to New Caledonia she sided with the indigenous Kanak people in their revolt against French colonial rule.

Lucy Parsons, a militant anarchist and trade unionist of mixed African-American and Cree heritage, was born in the United States in 1853, possibly a slave. Her husband (and fellow anarchist organizer) Albert Parsons was incriminated in the Haymarket Affair in Chicago, when a bomb exploded during a rally where workers were demanding an eight-hour day. Eight anarchists were convicted; seven were sentenced to death. Despite an international campaign for their pardon, the sentence was upheld for five of the anarchists. One committed suicide the night before his execution; the other four were hanged, including Albert Parsons. Lucy Parsons continued to be a prominent anarchist activist: she spoke alongside Kropotkin, wrote for several anarchist publications, and was one of the founders of the Industrial Workers of the World (iww).

Emma Goldman was born in Lithuania into a Jewish family of modest means. She immigrated to the United States and fell into poverty in New York. She became an anarchist, partly because of the hangings after the Haymarket Affair, and wrote for several anarchist newspapers. She was a tireless public speaker. One of her lovers, Alexander Berkman, also an anarchist, spent years in prison for his attempt to assassinate Henry Clay Frick, the head of Carnegie Steel, in 1892. Frick had cut the wages of his employees and sent Pinkerton guards to attack strikers, which resulted in the deaths of ten workers and three guards. Emma Goldman herself was imprisoned many times. She and Berkman were deported to Russia, where they were active for several years after the Bolshevik Revolution before returning to the United States.

Errico Malatesta, a famous Italian anarchist, travelled to several countries to help organize anarchist movements. He spent twelve years in Argentina, took part in uprisings in Spain and strikes in Belgium, and spent time in prisons in France, Britain, and Switzerland. He died while under house arrest in Italy during the fascist regime of Benito Mussolini. The writings of all these anarchist theoreticians were shaped by their experiences as militants, and by their discussions and debates with other activists.

THOMAS: Before we move on, here's another definition of anarchism that I came across. I wonder what you think of it. It's from a book called *Histoire de l'anarchisme* (History of anarchism) by Jean Préposiet: "Anarchism is essentially a state of mind, a way of being in the world, before it's a political position that can be classified and defined ... above all, it's a way of living and understanding reality." That makes it sound like anarchism is everything and anything, which I don't find very helpful.

FRANCIS: You have to understand that phrase "a way of living and understanding reality" from an anarchist perspective. As a definition, it's a little circular, I agree. But what it's really saying is that we can think and act in an anarchist way at all times and in all aspects of our lives. Because the fact is, some people make distinctions between different ways of being an anarchist, or different reasons for being one, or different ways of expressing anarchy in different contexts. Let's stop and look at some of those distinctions. The four most common are: political anarchism, cultural anarchism, social anarchism, and existential anarchism. Just remember: these are over-simplifications. Reality, as you and I know, is much more fluid and complex.

Political anarchism refers to the women and men who identify with anarchist ideology and the anarchist move-ment, people who are active in political groups. It's hard to actually know who's in the anarchist movement, because there's no membership list and no recognized affiliation. Research in the United States and France has shown that people become militant anarchists for different reasons. Often it's for love or friendship (in other words, when someone introduces you to the movement); or out of disil-lusionment with the hierarchical and authoritarian nature of other political groups (perhaps you've been kicked out of another group by people calling you an anarchist); or through the influence of books, pamphlets, and music.

Political anarchism varies in form and strength, depending on the time and place.

At the moment, it's strong in Greece, where it's breathing new life into the anti-austerity movement and the fight against racism and the extreme right. In Ger-many it's been well-established since the 1970s, under the name Autonomen. German anarchists have been active in squatting abandoned properties, fighting neo-Nazis and racists, and opposing nuclear power. In France, political anarchism comes under the umbrella of the Fédération anarchiste, which first appeared at the end of the Second World War. It publishes a journal, *Le Monde libertaire* (Libertarian world), and runs a bookstore in Paris and a radio station. There are other organizations, too, such as Alternative libertaire and dozens of independent collectives and networks of squats. In North America, anarchism is strongest in Quebec, though none of the organizations there have been around for more than a decade and most anarchists are active in social organizations or movements that don't claim to be anarchist. One exception would be l'Union communiste libertaire, though it isn't very active nowadays.

THOMAS: You're making this distinction called political anarchism. I thought anarchism was always political.

FRANCIS: Yes, of course it is. But I'm talking about a kind of anarchism that explicitly calls itself anarchist, and which is militant. There's also cultural anarchism, where an anarchist way of seeing the world finds expression in music, books, and other artistic activities. There are punk groups from the 1980s like Bérurier Noir and René Binamé; the latter sang old revolutionary songs from the nineteenth century. Or Léo Ferré and his songs about anarchism. There are anarchist book fairs in London, Montreal, Paris, and other cities. There are resource centres, such as Documentation, information, références et archives, in Montreal, and Centre international de recherche sur l'anarchisme (International centre for research on anarchism), in Lausanne and Marseille. These resource centres are an important part of anarchism, because they preserve historical memory, encourage activism, and celebrate activists. Then there are films that dramatize the lives of anarchists, such as *Land and Freedom* and *Libertaria*, about the Spanish Civil War. Anarchist academics are also part of cultural anarchism. Cultural anarchists often collaborate with political anarchists. They help organize benefit concerts and even get involved in political groups. The relationship between political anarchism and cultural anarchism is quite fluid. Remember, these distinctions really are oversimplifications.

Social anarchism refers to social movements and militant organizations that don't actually call themselves anarchists but which function in an anarchist way. Most radical feminist groups and environmental groups fall into this category. What they have in common is a collective approach to living and understanding reality. They organize themselves in a free and egalitarian manner, without leaders or hierarchy.

For example, during the long strike by Quebec students in 2012, activists in Montreal formed autonomous, grass-roots neighbourhood assemblies known as APAQS (Assemblées populaires autonomes de quartier). They weren't identified with any particular ideology. But as one participant told me, they were run in such a way that you "had the experience of anarchy without actually talking about anarchism." Another woman I spoke to, who was about seventy years old, put it this way: "Anarchism is a state of mind. I was an anarchist all my life, but I didn't know it. Now I'm proud to say I'm an anarchist." She'd been a militant socialist in Latin America in the 1970s, but discovered she was really an anarchist while participating in general assemblies of the Occupy movement in Montreal in 2011.

There have been popular neighbourhood assemblies

in many places—in Argentina in 2000, in Greece during the economic and political crisis of 2010. In a lot of slums, what appears at first glance to be chaos is in fact people helping one another and coordinating their efforts while remaining autonomous. There's a little book called *Anarchy in the Age of Dinosaurs*, written by the Curious George Brigade. It explains that mutual assistance and relationships based on giving freely are common in communities living in extreme poverty, in abandoned areas outside state control and beyond the reach of large private corporations. For example, an anthropologist studied a shanty town in Ghana and found that the practice of giving gifts there was essential for maintaining friendships, solidarity, and social relations, without which it was impossible to survive.

Finally, there are existential anarchists, people who are anarchists for psychological or moral reasons. Anarchism fits their way of being in the world. Some people by nature are more authoritarian, others more anarchist. Authority rubs some people the wrong way; they resist orders and constraints. Voltairine de Cleyre, a nineteenth-century American feminist, said she was an anarchist "because I cannot help it, I cannot be dishonest with myself." She added: "The instinct of liberty naturally revolted not only at economic servitude, but at the outcome of it, class-lines."

Obviously, existential or psychological anarchism is a fuzzy notion. But some homeless people, and some women who were abused when they were girls, are highly resistant to any attempt to constrain them or force them to do something they don't want to do. Think of the main character in the film *Boxcar Bertha*, who's a hobo. These people illegally rode freight trains back and forth across the continent in the early years of the twentieth century, looking for freedom and adventure. They mingled with thieves and prostitutes, and they visited cafés run by anarchists. But it's difficult to explain why one person becomes an anarchist after experiencing life's difficulties, and another person becomes passive or even authoritarian. Having an anarchist personality doesn't necessarily lead to political engagement; it may come out in other ways.

To sum up, anarchy can be expressed when an individual refuses to obey an authority; or when a group of people organize themselves without a leader in order to help each other and act collectively; or when anarchist ideas are expressed in art and culture; or when people form a militant group and struggle in the name of anarchy.

But again, reality is often too complex and nuanced to fit these kinds of categories. For example, there was a counter-culture movement in Amsterdam in the mid-1960s called the Provos, part of the revival of anarchism after the Second World War. The Provos included many different kinds of people. There were young avant-garde artists who staged "happenings" in public to shock the bourgeoisie and the arts establishment; there were beatniks and hippies, influenced by the counter-culture movement in the United States, who smoked marijuana and took LSD; there were experienced militant anarchists who wrote for newspapers; there were rockers and hoodlums from disadvantaged neighbourhoods; and there were older intellectuals and artists who were sympathetic. All these people gathered together to take collective actions against the establishment, and together they suffered police repression.

Sometimes a single person embodies the different forms of anarchism, such as Maria Lacerda de Moura, a Brazilian woman born in 1877. She wrote for anarchist and trade union newspapers, was active in avant-garde anarchist theatre, marched for women's rights and better education for the working class, and helped start several women's anti-war committees and the International Women's Federation.

Power (Part I)

THOMAS: Let's not get bogged down in definitions, and carry on. I have some more questions. The dictionaries all seem to agree on the origin of the word "anarchy": from the Greek *an*, "without," and *arkos*, "chief or leader." But is it enough to talk about opposition to hierarchy? What about authority?

I've been doing some reading, and found this quote by Émile Armand, the pseudonym of Ernest-Lucien Juin. He wrote an essay in 1911 called "Petit manuel anarchiste individualiste" (Mini-manual of individualist anarchism). It says:

> To be an anarchist is to deny authority and reject its economic corollary: exploitation—and that in all the domains where human activity is exerted. The anarchist wishes to live without gods or masters; without patrons or directors; a-legal, without laws as without prejudices; amoral, without obligations as without collective morals. He wants to live freely, to live his own idea of life.

But it seems to me that if you talk about the absence of something, or abolishing something, in this case authority, then that thing first has to exist.

And here's another interesting quote, by Élisée Reclus, from 1894: "There were people opposed to power long before there were anarchists. . . . There have always been free men, men who have been contemptuous of the law, men living without masters, by the primordial right of their existence and their thought. . . . Anarchy is as old as humanity."

So, to understand anarchy, don't we have to understand the origins of power, to know when, how, and where power first arose? Did it begin with the very first man and woman wanting to control each other? Is that the origin of authority? And what do we really mean by power or authority? Is it simply the domination of one individual or group over another individual or group?

FRANCIS: There are really two questions here: what is authority, and when did it arise? I'll start with the first. As you pointed out, the word *anarchy* comes from the Greek, like most words for political systems. Monarchy is government by only one person (*monarkhia*). Aristocracy is government by a hereditary elite, the nobility (*aristo*-cracy). Democracy is government by the people (*demos*-cracy) or the majority. Anarchy basically means the absence of a leader or authority. The enemies of anarchy use the word negatively, to refer to a troublesome, chaotic, violent, or unlawful situation. The proponents of anarchy see the absence of a leader as positive, and necessary for genuine freedom and equality to exist. As soon as there's an authority, there is no freedom for those who must obey. Nor can there be equality when there are rulers and subordinates.

The work of Patricia Hill Collins, an African-American feminist, is helpful in understanding this. Collins is not an anarchist but studies systems of domination, such as capitalism and the state. She found that these systems have four distinct characteristics: domination, oppression, exploitation, and exclusion.

Domination means the power that one or more dominant people have to decide the norms, rules, privileges, duties, and prohibitions for the community. The dominant ones are those who order or command the others. For example, politicians, employers, or a "head of the household" are in positions not only of authority but also of domination.

Oppression is the act of forcing subordinates to obey the dominants and the norms, rules, privileges, duties, and prohibitions that the dominants want to impose. This is usually accomplished by violence or the threat of violence—in other words, by coercion. In terms of functions—who does what—the head of state is the dominant; the soldiers, police officers, judges, and prison guards are the oppressors. In some situations, the dominant and the oppressor are the same person, such as when the head of the household is also a violent man. In order to dominate his family and impose his will, he oppresses his wife and children with threats of violence ("Just you wait and see!" ... "I'll kill you!") or, if that doesn't work, with physical violence resulting in injuries.

THOMAS: So many words... don't they all amount to the same thing? *Government, authority, control, domination, power, oppression, exploitation, exclusion* — they all seem to add up to an individual or a system that wants to exercise some form of authority or power. What anarchists are rejecting is a system of hierarchy.

FRANCIS: Sure, you can look at it that way, because so far we've just been talking about the relationship of power between dominants and their subordinates. But material and economic interests are also at play. And that's why, when we talk about domination and oppression, we also have to look at exploitation, the process by which dominants and oppressors profit from the work of their subordinates — or, to put it another way, the time and labour that the subordinates devote to the profit of those who dominate them. If there were no dominants, the subordinates could work less and they wouldn't have to overproduce to satisfy the needs and desires of those at the top. Some systems of domination are extremely exploitative, such as slavery. But exploitation can also be invisible, when the work is done for free or "out of love," such as domestic work and parenting, which is mostly done by women.

It's all connected: through systems of domination the dominant people establish, formally or informally, the norms and rules that determine who works, at what task, and how the goods and services produced by the workers are allocated. Under the capitalist system, it's taken for granted that employers and managers know best how to organize the work, sell the goods and services produced, and distribute the profits (and losses). Under systems of male domination, called "the patriarchy," we are told

that society will function better if women do the tasks
said to correspond to their feminine nature and mater-
nal instinct, while men do tasks identified as masculine.
Men as a class exploit the domestic and parental labour of
women. Oppression happens when the woman doesn't do
what's expected of her: she may be insulted or assaulted
because dinner isn't on the table when the man wants it,
or it isn't to his taste.

Men also have the power to exploit women sexually,
both in a personal or family relationship, and in the
so-called sex industry. Anarchist women such as Voltairine de Cleyre and Emma Goldman, like their nineteenth century feminist predecessors, say there are two
kinds of prostitution: legal prostitution, within marriage,
where the woman receives shelter and other benefits in
exchange for sex; and paid prostitution, where the prostitutes exchange sex for money, one trick at a time. According to Goldman and de Cleyre, both forms of prostitution should be condemned, and women will only be truly
emancipated when they are free of both economic and
sexual exploitation.

Ultimately, every system of domination contains
structures of exclusion and segregation that are imposed
by the dominants on their subordinates. These structures
serve to exclude the subordinates from the spheres of
decision-making. Women are excluded from male occu-
pations, the poor are excluded from private property and
corporate boardrooms, etc.

While the definition of anarchy is generally negative, in
the sense that it rejects domination, it also envisions a positive model of social organization. Without domination,

in principle, there wouldn't be oppression, exploitation, or exclusion; there would be freedom, equality, and solidarity. The rejection of domination, the rejection of leaders, power, and authority, can find expression in all areas of human activity, even though anarchists are mainly preoccupied with critiquing domination by the state and exploitation by the bourgeoisie under capitalism.

THOMAS: That's all well and good, but when did it all begin? Because there must have been a first dominant, someone who wanted to exercise his authority, and someone else who rejected that authority. In the Judeo-Christian creation myth, Eve questioned God's authority, so she must have been the first anarchist.

FRANCIS: Eve, the first anarchist—I love it!

THOMAS: Well, the book of Genesis says: "And God said, Let us make man in our image, after our likeness: and let them have dominion over... every creeping thing that creepeth upon the earth." And if you look up *hierarchy* in the dictionary, it comes from the Greek word meaning "sacred ruler."

FRANCIS: In the Judeo-Christian myth, God was the original authority figure. God gave Adam, the first man, a share of his authority, but also ordered him not to bite into the apple of earthly paradise. The apple would have allowed Adam to distinguish between good and evil, and thus become morally autonomous. Eve disobeyed, which is another way of saying that she wanted to be morally free to choose between good and evil. In the Bible, God is not only a dominant but also an oppressor, because he takes violent and malicious revenge on anyone who disobeys him. He expels Adam and Eve from paradise. He forces Adam to work in order to feed himself. He condemns Eve to suffer pain in childbirth and to be dominated by her husband. You can see here the punitive logic of a supreme authority figure. But it doesn't end there: Adam goes on to become the first king and impose his authority on his descendants.

According to this creation myth, history begins with God's domination, and anarchy comes after, in the form of Eve reacting against God's domination. But it's just a story. Which means we could imagine it differently. If anarchism is not just a negation of authority, but also a positive proposition, why not imagine that the first human communities practiced anarchy from the start, without any pre-existing dominant authority? Why not believe that in the beginning was anarchy?

Anthropology

THOMAS: You don't have to be an anarcho-primitivist to recognize that, long before feudal times, there were societies that functioned, sometimes for millennia, without a political authority, without a state or police. Think of the Inuit, the Pygmies, the Santals in India, the Tivs in West Africa. They practiced autonomy, voluntary association, self-organization, mutual help, and direct democracy.

FRANCIS: Indeed. Anthropologists like Harold Barkley, Marshall Sahlins, Pierre Clastres, and David Graeber, and some of the late-nineteenth and early-twentieth century anarchists such as Élisée Reclus and Peter Kropotkin, have all pointed out that for most of human history people lived in libertarian and egalitarian communities, practicing mutual assistance and solidarity. Take for example the First Nations of North America, or even just those in the territory we now call Quebec, where you and I live. The "Indian chief," the guy with all the feathers in the cowboy films, certainly existed. But he was more like a community organizer than a leader. He tried to keep the community together and resolve conflicts by talking and setting a good example.

Nowadays, heads of states often operate above the law, or outside it. But we know from the accounts of the European settlers and colonialists that chiefs in North America were often the least well-off in their community. The chief didn't have the power to dominate and oppress: there was no police or prison. He didn't exploit his people; he had to share the spoils of war and the hunt, in order to keep the respect of his people and maintain his influence. And there was no political exclusion, since collective decisions were made through lengthy discussions in public. Everyone could participate, even women and children.

That's not to say that these Indigenous communities were perfect and without violence. The anthropologist Pierre Clastres, for one, has shown that libertarian and egalitarian communities worried constantly that individuals would succumb to a thirst for power and domination.

Laughter was often the best defence against the ambitious, because without coercive power, what can a pow-
er-hungry person do in the face of ridicule? If laughter
wasn't enough, then the community drove him into exile,
or sometimes killed him, claiming he was possessed by
devils.

A French soldier and explorer, Louis-Armand de Lom
d'Arce, baron de Lahontan, published a fascinating book in
1703. It's an account of his years living with the "savages"
in New France. Lahontan created a fictional character for
his book called Adario, a member of the Huron–Wendat
people, and imagined having a dialogue with him about
various social issues and things like religion and marriage.
Adario is surprised and disgusted by the political and social
system of the French who came and colonized the territory. How could they blindly obey their king? How could
they accept a justice system that was so lenient on the rich
and so cruel to the poor? Why do Europeans work so hard
to produce useless luxury goods rather than enjoy their
lives? Why do the poor consent to working themselves to
death for the benefit of the rich? How can the rich pass
the poor in the street without seeming to notice them, or
making the slightest effort to help them? Why do fathers
think they can prohibit their daughters from having sexual
relations or loving the man they choose, and order them
to marry someone else? All these practices of domination,
oppression, exploitation, and exclusion seemed absurd
and revolting to Adario.

THOMAS: Émile Armand says in his "Mini-Manual of
Individualist Anarchism": "The work of the anarchist is

above all a work of critique. The anarchist goes, sowing revolt against that which oppresses, obstructs, opposes itself to the free expansion of the individual being. He agrees first to rid brains of preconceived ideas, to put at liberty temperaments enchained by fear, to give rise to mindsets free from popular opinion and social conventions." What you were just saying about Native Americans certainly challenges the conventional view of humanity habitually submitting to structures of domination and to leaders.

FRANCIS: Peter Kropotkin took the idea even further in a book called *Mutual Aid: A Factor of Evolution*. He wrote it around 1900, after years spent working as a geographer. Kropotkin developed his political ideas in the liberal intellectual circles of the day, at a time when people were debating the social implications of Darwin's theory of evolution. Social Darwinism was an overly simplistic extrapolation from Darwin's theory of natural selection. Social Darwinists used the theory to argue that competition, both political and economic, and the struggle of one against all, was coded in our genes and therefore had to be accepted. The idea justified the militarization of the state, war, colonialism, capitalism, employers, and even the patriarchy and the church.

But Kropotkin was more impressed by a lecture he heard in 1880 titled "On the law of mutual assistance," given by a zoologist, a professor Kessler from the University of St. Petersburg. Kropotkin summarized Kessler's thesis like this: "Kessler's idea was, that besides the Law of Mutual Struggle there is in Nature the law of Mutual Aid,

which, for the success of the struggle for life, and especially for the progressive evolution of the species, is far
more important than the law of mutual contest." Kropotkin argued that Darwin's theory had been misinterpreted.
His reading of *On the Origin of Species* turned up numerous
passages showing the importance of cooperation.

A Darwin expert, David Loye, confirmed this many
years later. Loye noted that in Darwin's later book, *The
Descent of Man*, there are only two mentions of "survival of
the fittest," one of them Darwin's acknowledgement that
he overstated its importance in *On the Origin of Species*.
In contrast, Loye found twenty-four mentions of mutual
assistance, sixty-one mentions of sympathy for others, and
ninety mentions of morality. Kropotkin himself pointed
out that in *The Descent of Man*, Darwin said: "Those communities which included the greatest number of the most
sympathetic members would flourish best, and rear the
greatest number of offspring."

Kropotkin's thinking on this developed during a geo-
graphical expedition to Siberia, where he observed that
the plant and animal species that had adapted best to the
harsh environment were those that practised mutual assistance. Kropotkin went on to study human communities
in their historical context all over the world. He found
that many communities practised mutual assistance and
functioned in a more or less libertarian and egalitarian
manner. In Europe as late as the Middle Ages, society still
operated largely on the basis of freedom, equality, and
solidarity.

Certainly, there were kings and nobles who appeared
to dominate a territory and its people. Their primary

function, however, was to ensure the defence of the territory and to organize large public works, such as draining
swamps. Most of the time the king and the nobles were
content to live on their estates, host parties, hunt, plan
expensive wars, and impose the taxes and conscription
needed to wage war. The ordinary people had little contact with the king or nobles.

In the countryside, thousands of small communities governed themselves through local assemblies. The
people debated and decided among themselves things of
common interest: how to manage their communal fields
and forests, how to organize the harvest and festivals, how
to care for the poor and destitute, how to hire teachers for
the village school, and, if wolves or thieves had been spot-
ted in the area, how to organize local security. In the cities,
merchant and craft guilds decided on prices, methods of
production, standards of quality, how to train apprentices,
and how to help injured or bankrupt members. That was
how the peoples of Europe governed themselves for centuries. After the Middle Ages, the state gradually suppressed
these liberties, banning guilds and village assemblies, and
nationalizing or privatizing resources that had previously
been owned and shared locally.

Kropotkin came to the conclusion that mutual assistance is both natural and favourable to evolution, and that
communities can sustain themselves for centuries, even
millennia, by living according to these principles. On the
other hand, he believed, struggle and competition invite
servitude, destruction, and death.

If we really think about what Kropotkin is saying, we
can let go of all those preconceived liberal notions about

how humans are and always will be essentially selfish and in competition with one another.

Human Nature

THOMAS: Kropotkin specifically drew a parallel between the animal and human worlds in an essay he wrote in 1898 called *Anarchist Morality*: "what is considered as good among ants, marmots, and Christian or atheist moralists is that which is *useful* for the preservation of the race; and that which is considered *evil* is that which is *hurtful* for race preservation. Not for the individual . . . but fair and good for the whole race." But that takes us back to the age-old question: is man inherently good or evil? If we're naturally good, then we can go off and live on kibbutzim, those cooperative, leaderless communities in Israel where decisions are made in general assemblies and where secularism and gender equality reign; or we can find some other self-governing commune to join somewhere else, one based on freedom and mutual aid, where people are trying to get away from the authority of the state. But if man is inherently evil and domineering, then we'll have to get rid of the weakest among us. Kropotkin has something to say about that, too:

> The distinction . . . between egoism and altruism is absurd in our eyes. . . . If this opposition were real, if the interests of the individual man were really opposed to those of society, the human race could never have come

into being; no animal species could have attained to its present development. . . . But never at any epoch, historical or even geological, have individual interests been in opposition to those of society.

FRANCIS: Why does it have to be one or the other? Let's acknowledge that we're a little of both. What's important is to cultivate the good in us, and suppress the evil. Most of the time, anarchists don't look at these questions in terms of individual personality; they take a sociological and structuralist approach. It's how society is organized and how individuals are socialized that determines whether good or evil gains the upper hand. Anarchism offers a moral vision—that the individual can improve and aspire to an ideal morality. But he can also regress and let his dark side take over. Even some anarchists regress, and thirst for power and privilege.

Where we have the most to fear is when a selfish individual gets into a position of authority that allows him to dominate, oppress, and exploit others. Anarchist writings are full of reflections on this subject. What really discourages me is when I'm giving a talk on anarchism and someone throws in my face, "Oh sure, anarchy would be great. But I saw a documentary about apes and it showed there's an alpha male in every community." As if that proves that equality can never exist. As if anarchists have never thought about why some individuals become powerful, and the relationship between power and personality. In fact, anarchists never stop thinking about these political issues. We're almost obsessed with them.

Louise Michel said "power makes one ferocious, egotistical and cruel; servitude is equally degrading." Reclus said "great men have more opportunities than everyone else to take advantage of their situation." He added, pessimistically, "from the moment a man is provided with any kind of authority, whether religious, military, administrative, or financial, his natural inclination is to make the most of it, without restraint." Bakunin said of political leaders: "The best, the purest, the most intelligent, the most disinterested, the most generous, will always and certainly be corrupted by this profession. How could they avoid *contempt for the popular masses and the exaggeration of their own merit?*" By the way, research in social psychology seems to show that the higher a person's social class, the more likely the person is to behave unethically, disrespect social rules, lie and cheat for their own profit, and be less altruistic and generous.

THOMAS: The British historian Lord Acton said it well: "Power tends to corrupt; absolute power corrupts absolutely."

FRANCIS: In the same vein, Kropotkin said: "Far from living in a world of visions and imagining men better than they are, we see them as they are; and that is why we affirm that the best of men is made essentially bad by the exercise of authority." Kropotkin could be sarcastic about those who believe that governments are good for us, an illusion he parodied as "pretty government and paternal utopia" in which

the employer would never be the tyrant of the worker;
he would be the father! ... Never would a public pros-
ecutor ask for the head of the accused for the unique
pleasure of showing off his oratorical talent ... and permanent armies would be the joy of citizens, as soldiers
would only take up arms to parade before nursemaids."

Anarchists know that within their own collectives
there's always a risk that an ambitious person might
gain influence and acquire privileges at the expense of
their comrades. Kropotkin was even wary of anarchists
themselves:

> We have not two measures for the virtues of the gov-
> erned and those of the governors; we know that *we our-
> selves are not without faults* and that the best of us would
> soon be corrupted by the exercise of power. We take
> men for what they are worth — and that is why we hate
> the government of man by man.

Anarchists have developed several strategies within
their organizations to reduce the possibility of individuals taking too much power. Anarchist collectives have
no official positions of authority, and tasks are usually
done voluntarily, for no pay. Positions of responsibility
are rotated, especially prominent positions such as public
spokesperson. Some groups publish texts anonymously, to
avoid personalizing ideas and to ensure that no individual
enjoys the prestige of publication. Other groups sign their
texts collectively or designate several spokespersons, to
avoid the appearance of a single leader and spokesperson.
Meetings are often chaired by two people rather than one;

their job is to ensure that everyone has a chance to speak
and no one dominates the discussion. So you see, anarchists find creative ways to ensure that their principles
are respected within their own organizations, including
in the process of decision-making and the transition from
consensus to collective action. Every anarchist collective
is different: each evolves in its own way as it encounters
new problems, absorbs new information and experiences,
and generates new ideas from within its own ranks.

THOMAS: I see what you mean: anarchist groups have to
make a special effort to prevent any member from even
seeming to wield authority over the others. No one can
have even an ounce of power!

FRANCIS: Yes, and that's equally true when it comes to
deciding on tactics. Anarchists are active in the Quebec
anti-capitalist alliance called Convergence des luttes
anti-capitalistes (Anti-Capitalist Convergence). In 2000
they decided to create a framework for street demonstrations based on the idea of liberty, equality, and solidarity.
The Quebec anarchists developed the concept of "respect
for a diversity of tactics." Prior to a demonstration, the
participants agree on zones: actual streets or areas in
the city are set aside for different kinds of protest. For
example, a red zone is designated for those who want
to confront the police or smash the windows of banks,
government offices, military recruitment centres, etc.; a
yellow zone is for those who want to practice nonviolent
civil disobedience; and a green zone is where people are
encouraged to demonstrate peacefully, or where they can

go to rest. (Obviously, the police don't always respect the boundaries between these zones.) The point is to not impose a single way of thinking and acting on everyone who wants to demonstrate.

Liberty and equality are principles that need the right environment and sufficient structure to blossom and grow. Anarchists are not naive. On the contrary, it's precisely because anarchists are realistic and pessimistic that they don't want leaders. If human beings were naturally good, there'd be no problem having leaders, since they'd always be good and would never abuse their power. But anarchists know that's not going to happen. So they organize themselves in the most egalitarian way possible, without creating positions of power. They hope that will encourage human beings to cooperate and help each other.

Kropotkin said that a tension between the instinct of domination (oppression, exploitation, exclusion) and the instinct of autonomy (liberty, equality, solidarity, and mutual assistance) exists in each individual and in every community, and these opposite poles are in permanent conflict. He wrote:

> Throughout the history of our civilization, two traditions, two opposing tendencies have confronted each other: ... the authoritarian and the libertarian. ... Between these two currents, always manifesting themselves, always at grips with each other—the popular trend and that which thirsts for political and religious domination—we have made our choice.

THOMAS: Which do you think has the upper hand today,

selfishness or mutual aid? In Western societies things seem to have swung radically to the side of individualism and selfishness.

FRANCIS: You're right. The anthropologist Marshall Sahlins has shown that individualism is one of the distinguishing features of our civilization. Yet, throughout history, almost everywhere in the world, selfish, ambitious individualism has been considered a kind of pathology and a problem, and the selfish individual a danger to oneself and others. Sahlins explains that

> for the greater part of humanity, self-interest as we know it is unnatural in the normative sense: it is considered madness, witchcraft or some such grounds for ostracism, execution or at least therapy. Rather than expressing a pre-social human nature, such avarice is generally taken for a loss of humanity.

Instead, the social norm in families and communities should be a collective spirit of generosity, empathy, and solidarity.

THOMAS: Well, capitalist society is based on the enrichment of individuals, rather than the community. One of the primary concerns of the so-called modern state is to reconcile capitalism and socialism, which seems a contradiction, if not impossible. Take for example the former socialist government of François Hollande, in France. He tried to impose a ceiling on the salaries and bonuses of the highest earners, but at the same time he imposed more and more financial burdens on the poor. The result was that the gap between rich and poor was maintained, and low-income people saw no increase in their purchasing power.

FRANCIS: All this discussion about whether humans are inherently good or evil is a slippery slope to an ideological justification of the state. Among other things, the state is supposed to protect us from the worst effects of the free market. We have convinced ourselves that we can no longer trust our neighbours, not even our brother, since we're all selfish individualists and everyone is a threat. Therefore we need the state and the police to protect us from everyone else. What's left out of the equation is who will protect us from the state and its police. If the state and the police are composed of selfish individualists, which is probably the case since to get to the top of the pyramid you have to be ambitious, then we are truly screwed. To be a leader you have to crave power and want to dominate others, and that's why leaders are necessarily a threat.

Metaphysics

THOMAS: I've been asking you questions about the meaning of words like *authority*, *leader*, and *hierarchy*. You've given me a kind of nomenclature of the different forms of domination, and some insight into where they began. All this leads me to other questions, ones I should perhaps have started with. The fundamental question is this: within the domains of the plant kingdom, the mineral kingdom,

and the animal kingdom, is there a "natural" hierarchy? If
not then anarchy, or the absence of hierarchy, must be the
natural state of the world.

FRANCIS: To answer that question we have to examine
our ontological beliefs, in other words, our ideas about
the nature and essence of being and the origin of the
cosmos. Vivien Garcia published a book in France called
L'anarchisme aujourd'hui (Anarchism today), which looks
at precisely those big metaphysical questions. But he also
points out that some anarchists have no interest in defin-
ing a metaphysics or an anarchist ontology, because to do
so, they say, would necessarily be authoritarian and would
lead, somewhat arbitrarily, to the exclusion of those who
don't share the same ideas about the world and nature.
It's entirely possible to be an anarchist without worrying
about ontological questions or metaphysics. That said,
some anarchists insist that anarchism is a principle found
in nature, both in the microcosm and the macrocosm.

According to Garcia, several famous nineteenth-century anarchists, including Proudhon, Bakunin and Max
Stirner, believed that nature and society are in continuous
transformation, and that it's the contradictory impulses in
both which provide the impetus for change. The sociologist Daniel Colson says that the very notion of anarchy
evokes the chaos, and the absence of authority and absolute
unity, in nature and in life itself. Hence, Colson argues,
anarchy is already present in both nature and society.

Seen from this perspective, nothing exists in and for
itself; nothing is wholly unique, complete in itself, and
isolated from everything else. There are no monads, that

is, beings or things that are completely homogeneous, which are not composed of other beings or things. On the contrary, every being or thing is necessarily the result of other beings or things, and is therefore influenced by other beings or things, which both compose it, on the inside, and surround it, as an environment. Some of these influences can be negative, leading to destruction and death; others are positive, fostering growth and life. But beings and things are in constant transformation and continue to be part of reality even after their destruction or death. In short, there is no stable and permanent order, everything is always changing or potentially changing, and so there is always the possibility of change.

Let me read you something Bakunin wrote about nature. This is how he begins his essay called "Considérations philosophiques sur le fantôme divin, le monde réel et l'Homme" (Philosophical considerations on the divine ghost, the real world, and man):

> Nature is the sum of all things that have real existence.... Things that exist today will not exist tomorrow. Tomorrow they will not pass away but will be entirely transformed. Therefore I shall find myself much nearer to the truth if I say: Nature *is the sum of actual transformations of things that are and will ceaselessly be produced within its womb.* ... All this boundless multitude of particular actions and reactions, combined in one general movement, produces and constitutes what we call Life, Solidarity, Universal Causality, Nature.... Thus defined, this Universal Solidarity, Nature viewed as an infinite universe, is imposed upon our mind as a rational necessity.

Bakunin's conception of the universe is anarchist and anarchic. But as I said before, that doesn't mean you have to take an interest in these kinds of philosophical notions in order to be an anarchist. Essentially, what Bakunin is saying is that there is no authority which orders the natural world; everything is both autonomous and at the same time connected, everything is influencing and being influenced by other things. What's more, everything is in some sense possible, even if we ourselves cannot grasp all the possibilities afforded by this absolute freedom. And because everything is connected and in mutual relationship to other things, it's also possible to understand this apparent chaos as an anarchy that is ordered, in the sense that my freedom is in part influenced by the relationships that I have with other freedoms, and vice versa.

THOMAS: OK, so we live in a world that is totally anarchic, in the sense that it's chaotic. But can we bring this back to the human level, to the level of the individual? Because it seems to me that anarchists always act as individuals. They don't follow a party line or a movement, except perhaps during the Russian and Spanish revolutions.

FRANCIS: Don't worry, I'm getting there. But first I want to delve a little deeper into the anarchist view of nature. In the late nineteenth and early twentieth centuries, scientific knowledge was advancing rapidly. A lot of anarchists believed that science was not only compatible with an anarchist view of the world, but that it was possible to scientifically prove the superiority of anarchism. In 1901

Kropotkin published a book called *Modern Science and Anarchism*. In it he declared, somewhat pompously, that

> Anarchism is a world-concept based upon a mechanical explanation of all phenomena, embracing the whole of Nature — that is, including in it the life of human societies and their economic, political, and moral problems. Its method of investigation is that of the exact natural sciences. . . . Its aim is to construct a synthetic philosophy comprehending in one generalization all the phenomena of Nature — and therefore also the life of societies. . . .

A similar idea shows up in Élisée Reclus, a self-declared anarchist and one of the most influential geographers of the late-nineteenth century. He wrote a book called *L'évolution, la révolution et l'idéal anarchique* (Evolution, revolution, and the anarchist ideal) in which he says: "Evolution is the infinite movement of all that exists, the incessant transformation of the universe and all its parts since its eternal origins and through the infinity of ages. . . . " He adds: "It's by myriads and myriads that revolutions succeed one other in the universal evolution; yet, negligible as [revolutions] are, they are part of this infinite movement. Thus science sees no contradiction between these two words — Evolution and Revolution."

This view of nature is entirely consistent with anarchist political ideas. When anarchists criticize authority and the conservative, authoritarian defence of social order, their argument is based on a view of nature in which nothing lasts forever, nothing remains stable, everything is in flux, and everything is possible, meaning that even the slightest movement can be an evolution or even a revolution.

THOMAS: So, once again we're trying to explain the way the world evolves and therefore how society evolves. If I'm understanding you correctly, anarchy can be merely a reflection of that evolution, but sometimes it can be a contributing cause. Is that right?

FRANCIS: Exactly! Now, more recently, a philosopher of science named Paul Feyerabend, who died in 1994, published a book called *Against Method*. The original French publisher added a provocative subtitle, *Outline of an Anarchist Theory of Knowledge*. Feyerabend argues that the established method of teaching the history of science is really a brainwashing operation, because it wants us to believe that science develops in a rational, logical, linear fashion. Feyerabend argues instead that developments in scientific and technological knowledge happen largely thanks to individuals who do not respect the established norms of their times, people who dare to break the rules of their discipline and who resist the most commonly received dogmas and the experts who espouse them. He says: "Science is an essentially anarchist enterprise: theoretical anarchism is more humanitarian and more likely to encourage progress than its law-and-order alternative." Putting aside the fact that chance and accidents also sometimes provide breakthroughs in knowledge, the question then becomes: why is science better served by an anarchist approach than by respect for scientific norms and dogma? Because, Feyerabend argues, the world is largely "unknown": we don't know what we are looking for, and what's there waiting for us to discover. "Anarchism helps to achieve progress in any one of the senses one cares to choose," Feyerabend says.

As I've said, many anarchists don't worry about these kinds of questions. They're interested in human beings, in social relationships and the organization of communities. Vivien Garcia talks about the audacity of the French anarchist painter Gustave Courbet, who made a painting of a naked woman lying on a bed with her legs open, genitals exposed, and titled it *The Origin of the World*. Though we humans make all kinds of grandiose claims about our origins — created by God or the Big Bang, descended from a long line of dragon slayers or a magnificent nation — the truth is both simple and more complex: we enter the world naked and vulnerable. It's not authority that saves us, it's our mothers and fathers, and the adults who welcome us into their community. It's mutual aid, from the very beginning of our life, that allows us to survive.

Violence and Terrorism

THOMAS: And yet, when most people think of an anarchist, it's not mutual aid that comes to mind. It's a guy with a beard and a clenched fist, throwing a bomb.

FRANCIS: First, I want to thank you for not starting off this whole discussion by asking me if it's true that anarchists plant bombs, burn grandmothers, and eat children. Any serious examination of the relationship between anarchists and violence would show that the state commits far more violence against anarchists than vice versa. Again and again throughout history, the state has imprisoned,

tortured, and executed anarchists, sometimes individually, sometimes en masse. So have extreme right-wing
militias, for example the Patriotic League in Argentina
and the fascists in Europe. And it's still happening. In the
United States, Canada, and France, anarchists are the
most oppressed political activists, on a par perhaps with
"Islamists." Generally speaking, the state and capitalism,
and even sexism and racism, are much more violent and
deadly than anarchists have ever been.

THOMAS: I can see I touched a nerve. But the fact remains
that the stereotype of the bomb-throwing anarchist has
taken root in the public's mind. When I googled for names
of anarchists who've killed, I came across Ravachol, Bonnot, and Sacco and Vanzetti. What pops up much more
often are the names of people who've been assassinated or
targeted by anarchists, such as President McKinley of the
United States and King Umberto I of Italy.

FRANCIS: If this stereotype of the anarchist weren't so
pernicious, I'd suggest we move on to more important
things right away. But it needs to be addressed. Unfortunately, discussions about anarchism and even books about
anarchism often begin with this association between anarchism and bomb-throwing. It's strange, really, because
books about liberalism and republicanism never begin
by saying that liberal and republican regimes began with
violence, with the beheading of kings, revolutions, civil
wars, or colonies.

Instead we're told that republicanism began in Ancient
Rome, that it developed in cities such as Florence and

Venice during the Renaissance, appeared in Holland and England in the seventeenth century, and then in France in the eighteenth century. We're told that the great minds of the American independence movement gave rise to modern-day republicanism and the founding of the United States of America in 1787. We're asked to believe that republicanism in France was the product of great French minds who spread their ideas in the literary salons of Paris. We're told that an essential characteristic of republicanism is the virtue of citizenship, defined as love of the common good and of one's country, and the participation of citizens in public affairs—the first duty being readiness for military sacrifice to protect the Republic (or, for women, giving birth to future soldiers and teaching them respect for the Republic).

Liberalism is presented as a philosophy that arose in Great Britain in the seventeenth century, in opposition to the monarchy and the church. Liberalism, we're told, is expressed in values (autonomy, pluralism, and tolerance), in politics (respect for the rights of individuals), in economics (the "free market," the right of private property, and the system of wage earning) and in culture (freedom of expression and creation). All this, we are told, but the word *violence* is never mentioned.

Some even rewrite history by reducing these movements to pure ideas. They say that it's thanks to the great ideas of liberalism that women and slaves were emancipated in the late nineteenth and early twentieth centuries. They neglect to mention that women had to organize and demand their rights, and sometimes resort to violence to achieve them. In Great Britain, the most powerful and

influential country at the beginning of the twentieth century, suffragettes disrupted political meetings, organized
hundreds of vigils and protest marches, and vandalized
dozens of businesses in London. More than a thousand
suffragettes were imprisoned and many of them went on
hunger strikes. The suffragettes committed hundreds
of arson and bomb attacks in 1913 and 1914. Who talks
about that, these days?

Anarchism has to explain itself for a few bombs thrown
in the late nineteenth century, but republicanism and liberalism shrug off all responsibility for slavery, colonialism,
racism, and sexism. State governments are responsible for
wars that have killed millions of people. It was a liberal,
republican government in the United States that dropped
atomic bombs on two cities, killing hundreds of thousands
of civilians. But whole books are written about liberalism
without ever mentioning the atomic bomb, while every
book on anarchism seems to begin by talking about a few
anarchists who threw homemade bombs.

Why are so many people worried about anarchist
"terrorism" these days, when the political theory of
tyrannicide, which justifies killing a tyrant for the common good, was first developed in the West by devout
Christians? Monks assassinated several kings at the end
of the Middle Ages. And think of all the heads of state
who have been assassinated by terrorists who were *not*
anarchists. President Abraham Lincoln was assassinated
by a member of the Democratic Party. Emperor Yoshihito
of Japan was the target of two assassination attempts, the
first by a communist in 1923, then a year later by a Korean
separatist. We don't know who killed President John F.

Kennedy, but no one suspects it was an anarchist. In 1994, a plane carrying the presidents of Burundi and Rwanda was shot down by a missile. There, too, it doesn't seem to have been an anarchist attack. Anti-abortion activists in the United States have firebombed abortion clinics and murdered nurses and doctors, but we don't call those Christians "terrorists." Nationalists have murdered heads of state and planted bombs, but we don't associate nationalism with terrorism.

THOMAS: It's hard to tell the difference, sometimes, between nationalism, terrorism, and anarchism, or between revolution and anarchy.

FRANCIS: Uri Eisenzweig, a professor at Rutgers University in the United States, studied anarchist terrorism in France at the end of the nineteenth century. In his book *Fictions de l'anarchisme* (Anarchist fictions), Eisenzweig says that anarchism was denounced by the French media and repressed by the state even before there were any deaths caused by anarchists. The media claimed that anarchists were going to burn down Paris, and French politicians passed laws criminalizing not only violent acts committed in the name of anarchism, but also anarchist propaganda, on the grounds that anarchist ideas might inspire violence. Eisenzweig says these laws marked a new way of thinking about the power of ideas and gave birth to the image of the intellectual as someone who influences society and individual behaviour solely through words and writing. Seen in that light, anarchist propagandists were arguably the first modern intellectuals.

Of course, some anarchists think it's permissible to use force to defend or spread one's ideas. And there are anarchists who have committed violence in response to repression, such as when strikers are attacked by police. But when that happens, shouldn't it be the political leaders who are punished, for ordering a violent attack in the first place?

Mike Davis published a collection of essays called *Les héros de l'enfer* (The heroes of hell). He says the era of what anarchists call "propaganda of the deed" began in 1878 with several milestone events. French republican forces defeated the Paris Commune, executing about thirty thousand Communards in the process. A horrific campaign of judicial and police repression continued in France for years. Germany banned all socialist propaganda. Dozens of newspapers were shut down, public meetings were banned, and trade unions were dissolved. The justification for the law was two unsuccessful assassination attempts against Kaiser Wilhelm I, by the anarchists Max Hödel and Karl Nobiling. Also in 1878, King Alphonso XII of Spain escaped an assassination attempt by the anarchist Oliva Marcousi, and in Italy the anarchist Giovanni Passannante tried unsuccessfully to assassinate King Umberto I. In Russia, there were several failed assassination attempts against Tsar Alexander II; he was eventually killed three years later. In 1894, an Italian anarchist named Sante Geronimo Caserio assassinated the president of France, Sadi Carnot, in Lyon. Three years later, Michele Angiolillo killed the prime minister of Spain, Antonio Cánovas del Castillo. The following year Luigi Lucheni assassinated Empress Elizabeth of Austria.

In 1900, another anarchist succeeded in killing the Italian king Umberto I.

Around this time, several biological theories were put forward in an attempt to explain the murderous character of anarchists. Their skulls and facial features were analyzed, and their personalities described as selfish, antisocial, and short-tempered.

During the 1930s, anarchists tried to assassinate several European dictators: Mussolini in 1931 and 1932, Salazar in 1937, and Hitler in 1938. An anarchist tried to assassinate Raul Castro, the brother of Cuban President Fidel Castro, who had risen to high office after the Cuban Revolution. Sometimes, vengeance was the motive for anarchist violence. For example, in Argentina in 1923 an anarchist named Kurt Gustav Wilckens killed a colonel named Varela who had ordered the mass shooting of fifteen hundred workers and peasants during a labour uprising in Patagonia. Wilckens was himself murdered in prison by an Argentinian nationalist, Pérez Millán, who was in turn killed in prison by an anarchist. Around the same time, also in Argentina, the anarchist Pedro Espelocin tried to kill a foreman who mistreated a child.

Nowadays, there are almost no anarchists engaged in armed struggle. There was a group called the Angry Brigade in Britain in the early 1970s. And in Greece two groups emerged early in this century, Revolutionary Struggle and Conspiracy of Fire Nuclei, but most of their members are in prison.

The Black Bloc is the most widely known contemporary form of anarchist violence. But it's more a tactic than a group; it's a way of expressing a radical critique of

capitalism. People dress in black and wear masks to protest, and they confront police and smash bank windows.
But the violence is mainly symbolic, because it doesn't
stop the functioning of the financial system.

THOMAS: It's interesting to observe how the media cover
demonstrations. They spend more time reporting on the
violence, or the potential for violence, than covering the
reasons for the demonstration. The experts they quote are
usually former police officers who say "the police are only
doing their jobs" and "law and order have to be respected."
The height of absurdity is the annual 15 March demonstration against police brutality in Montreal, which inevitably leads to more police brutality.

FRANCIS: What's more, the police and the intelligence
services unduly exaggerate the threat posed by some
militant groups, claiming they are terrorists, or potential
terrorists, just so they can arrest them and subject them
to long, expensive judicial proceedings. That's what happened to the Tarnac Nine in France in 2008. The intelligence services inflamed the public's fear of an anarcho-
autonomist movement, then the police staged a dramatic,
middle-of-the-night arrest of about twenty people, accus-
ing them of planning to cut off the electricity to a railway
line. The police called them terrorists.

What's truly deplorable is when anarchist groups speak
out against such direct actions, and try to distance themselves from those arrested. If the motivation is to avoid
becoming targets of repression themselves, then it betrays
a flagrant lack of solidarity.

THOMAS: Well, anarchists don't always agree among themselves on the best ways to spread their ideas and fight authority. The sociologist you mentioned, Daniel Colson, argues that anarchist actions differ from terrorism in several ways. Anarchists are not trying to spread fear, he says, but to create a ripple effect, to spread revolt. Anarchist actions target the whole, rather than single out an ethnic or religious group. They are a spontaneous leap into action, not part of a rigid strategic plan. They are driven by a thirst for revolt, not the product of a hierarchical organization.

FRANCIS: Some anarchists deplore assassination. They say it's not an effective way to bring about social and political change, because it's too radical, too focussed on the individual, and can have dire consequences for the anarchist movement, not to mention the assassins themselves — it leads to the repression of all progressive forces, especially anarchists.

But there can be a political logic to assassination. It can be a response to repression, a way of communicating to the political and economic elite that they can't oppress the masses with impunity. Or it can be a way to destabilize an authoritarian regime, especially during times of mass terror, such as in Russia between 1902 and 1917, when there were twenty thousand attempted assassinations. And anarchist terrorism differs fundamentally from terrorism committed by other political groups — in an anarchist network or organization no one can order anyone else to carry out a particular action; the choice of violence or non-violence is individual, and voluntary.

Several well-known anarchists, including Voltairine de Cleyre, Emma Goldman, and Séverine, have spoken publicly in defence of assassins, and tried to explain their actions. The most dramatic example may be de Cleyre, who was herself the target of an assassination attempt by one of her students, who shot her three times at point-blank range. De Cleyre narrowly escaped death, yet refused to press charges against her attacker, on the grounds that he himself was the victim of difficult social conditions.

Goldman refused to condemn Leon Czolgosz for shooting President McKinley. She said that anarchism wasn't to blame for the violence; rather, it was liberal society's structural inequalities between those who govern and the governed, and between the rich and the poor. The inequalities, Goldman argued, incited despair and rage. "Anarchism does create rebels. Out of the blindly submissive, it makes the discontented; out of the unconsciously dissatisfied, it makes the consciously dissatisfied." Goldman publicly quoted Czolgosz's last words: "I killed the President because he was the enemy of the good people — the good working people."

Goldman also defended her lover, Alexander Berkman, who shot the industrialist Henry Clay Frick after he hired hundreds of goons to attack striking workers. Goldman later wrote an essay called "The Psychology of Political Violence" in which she analyzed several assassination attempts by, or attributed to, anarchists. She argued that anarchist resistance to tyranny, and even tyrannicide itself, was justified because anarchism, more than any other political philosophy, respected human life and dignity. Berkman made the same argument in his book *Now and After: The ABC of Communist Anarchism*, pointing out that many non-anarchists have assassinated tyrants, and in those cases the assassin is usually celebrated as a champion of the people's freedom.

In the same vein, Séverine proclaimed that she stood "With the poor, always—in spite of their mistakes, their faults . . . in spite of their crimes!"

It's important to remember, however, that some anarchists rule out violence completely. They argue that anarchism requires non-violence as a fundamental principle, since violence against another individual is, by definition, authoritarian, and therefore dominating and oppressive.

History of the Anarchist Movement

THOMAS: To help me better understand anarchy, could you tell me who are the most important anarchists, or your favourite anarchists, and a little about what they fought against and how they went about it?

FRANCIS: Let's not get caught up in the idea of anarchist superstars. Anarchism is a popular social movement kept alive by the work and commitment of countless anonymous individuals.

THOMAS: Fair enough. But the fact remains that many of the theoreticians of anarchy came from the educated elite. Kropotkin came from an aristocratic family!

FRANCIS: So did Bakunin. In anarchist networks, the
theoreticians are often militants, and vice versa. These
days, many anarchists come from the educated middle
and upper classes. Others are trying to rise in the social
hierarchy by going to university to get the skills and
qualifications to become professionals. That said, some
anarchists are writing theoretical and analytical texts from
outside the university. You can find their ideas online and
in pamphlets and newspapers.

Historically, several famous anarchist theoreticians
came from a humble or poor background with no intellectuals in their families. Proudhon came from an impoverished peasant family and had to quit school to help support
his parents. Emma Goldman arrived in the United States
from Russia without a penny to her name, and struggled
to earn a living. Even Kropotkin and Bakunin, sons of
the Russian aristocracy, couldn't avoid persecution and
prison, and died quite poor.

If you forget the big names for a moment, and look at
the broader anarchist movement that was born in Europe
in the nineteenth century, you'll see that anarchism was
part of the working-class revolutionary movement that
arose in reaction to capitalism and rapid industrialization.
The latter created a whole host of problems as masses of
people moved from the countryside to the cities, where
they ended up living in crowded, unhealthy slums such as
the East End of London, selling their labour for a mouth-
ful of bread. In the Swiss Jura, anarchism started among
watchmakers. In other countries, such as Russia, Italy, and
Spain, where agricultural capitalism was more powerful
and influential than industrial capitalism, anarchists were

especially active in peasant movements that tried to protect communal lands from the greed of private landowners supported by the state and the church. In most countries, anarchism, or at least a preference for autonomous self-management and a mistrust of political institutions such as parliaments and parties, was the most influential current of thought in the revolutionary movement of the nineteenth century. There were exceptions, for example Russia, where Marxism-Leninism came to the fore in the early twentieth century, with results that we're all familiar with.

The early anarchists were opposed to the bourgeoisie, the big landowners, capitalism, the state, and the church. While waiting for the revolution, they practiced mutual aid, formed revolutionary labour unions, and fought for better working conditions and a better life for the working class. Around 1870, anarchists helped form revolutionary labour unions in Russia, Egypt, Spain, the United States, Mexico, Cuba, and Uruguay.

These unions were particularly active among sailors and dock workers in port cities. It was there that workers from all over the world rubbed shoulders with deserters, adventurers, vagabonds, and prostitutes. It was in the port cities that news and information spread about revolts or repressions going on elsewhere in the world, as people fleeing tyranny and hoping to immigrate passed through the harbours. You should read *The Many-Headed Hydra: Sailors, Slaves, Commoners, and the Hidden History of the Revolutionary Atlantic*, by Marcus Rediker and Peter Linebaugh. It explains the important role of harbours in the spread of revolts in Britain's Atlantic colonies during the seventeenth and eighteenth centuries. The process intensified after 1870 with the onset of what some people regard as the "first globalization." On the west coast of the United States, for example, anarchists exiled from Japan and India exchanged ideas with American anarchists, later returning home to carry on the struggle.

Anarchism also spread along migration routes. At the beginning of the twentieth century, millions of Jews left Russia to escape anti-Semitic pogroms and the political repression that followed the failure of the 1905 revolution. They were mostly poor farmers and small businessmen, and many were sympathetic to anarchism. According to the sociologist Michael Löwy, there is an affinity between some anarchist ideas and certain tenets of Judaism, such as messianism, the belief that paradise can be created on Earth if we act here and now. The Jews then were a people without a state, which also aligns with anarchism. Many well-known anarchists were Jews, such as Emma Goldman and Gustav Landauer. So was the writer Franz Kafka, who frequented anarchist circles in Prague, including the Klub Mladých (Young People's Club), an anarchist, anti-militarist, and anti-clerical organization for young people. Kafka also participated in demonstrations and attended anarchist conferences.

On the other hand, some anarchists became anti-Semitic, especially following the Second World War when, for some, opposition to Zionism justified revisionism about the Holocaust. But even before that, in 1847, Proudhon wrote in his *Notebooks*:

> Write an article against this race that poisons everything by sticking its nose into everything without ever mixing with any other people. Demand its expulsion from

France with the exception of those individuals married to French women. . . . The Jew is the enemy of human-kind. They must be sent back to Asia or be exterminated. By steel or by fire or by expulsion the Jew must disap-pear. . . . Hatred of the Jew, as of the Englishman, needs to be an article of our political faith.

Proudhon also wrote hundreds of pages purporting to prove the physical, intellectual, and moral inferiority of women. Needless to say, I pass him over when I feel like picking up an anarchist author to read. I only consult Proudhon when I need to remind myself that anarchists can still be racist or misogynist.

In any case, waves of Jewish emigration from Russia and eastern Europe helped sow anarchist ideas in England, Argentina, the Marais district of Paris, Brooklyn in New York City, and in Montreal around Boulevard St-Laurent. Jewish anarchists published newspapers, often in Yiddish, and opened bookstores, libraries, and community centres providing adult education and mutual aid services. These immigrants, including women, often ended up working in the manufacturing sector, where they organized militant labour unions. These waves of migration were driven by poverty, political upheaval, and anti-semitism.

THOMAS: That's interesting. I grew up in a Jewish family in France during the Nazi occupation, but I'd never really thought about the relationship between anti-semitism and domination. It's true that anti-semites talk about a "superior race" and "second-class citizens," but Jews and Zionists refer to themselves as "the chosen people." The same thing happened during the civil rights struggle in the United States—the Black Panthers were a lot like anarchists. They said that in order to solve the concrete problems faced by the poorest African-Americans, theory had to translate into action. If community work didn't produce results, then direct action had to be taken, within a legal framework. Some Black Panthers, however, ended up preaching violence.

FRANCIS: Yes, and we can talk later about the anarchist perspective on racism, in all its forms. But anarchists also took part in anti-colonial struggles in places like the Philippines. There are so many examples. The Italian anarchist Errico Malatesta was forcibly exiled after taking part in revolts by Italian peasants. He subsequently took part in the struggle against the British in Egypt in 1882, then helped militants in Spain and Argentina. And his ideas circulated. Malatesta's writings have been translated into Spanish, Portuguese, and Turkish, and were even read aloud by Cuban cigar makers in their workplace. A Russian revolutionary, Sergei Stepniak, helped start a clandestine organization called Land and Liberty, fought against the Turks in Bosnia, and joined Malatesta's peasant uprising in Italy. From there he returned to Russia, assassinated the head of the Russian secret police in 1878, and fled to London, where he died in a train accident.

In the late nineteenth and early twentieth centuries, almost everywhere in the West, workers won the right to an eight-hour day, thanks largely to anarchist unions. A key event in that struggle was the Haymarket Affair in Chicago. Anarchists were blamed for a bomb explosion at a labour demonstration on 4 May 1886, and executed. The trial gave birth to an international solidarity movement, and May First is now celebrated around the world as International Workers' Day, in commemoration of the Haymarket Affair.

In Europe, unions developed the strategy of the general strike. In Barcelona in 1919, a hydroelectric company called La Canadiense cut wages and laid off workers. The anarcho-syndicalist labour union CNT, which had 700,000 members, began a general strike in response. Martial law was imposed and thousands of people were imprisoned, but the general strike succeeded. The workers won all their demands: union recognition, the rehiring of fired workers, and an eight-hour workday.

So you see, anarchist actions have directly influenced the way we live our lives today, not to mention the very structure of capitalism. Anarchists dream of using the general strike to bring down the capitalist system or to prevent States from going to war.

Anarchists brought their political struggles with them when they migrated from Europe to South America. In Chile, fifty thousand people belonged to anarchist organizations in 1910, when the total population of the country was only three million. In Argentina in 1919, a strike organized by anarchists led to a week of rioting and repression, which left a thousand people dead and fifty thousand arrested; it became known internationally as La Semana Trágica, or the Bloody Week.

THOMAS: We've been focussing on Europe and the Americas, but we shouldn't forget that there have been

many anarchists in Asia, too. I've heard it said that Taoism
shares some ideas with anarchism.

FRANCIS: The first anarchist group in Japan was started
in 1907 by Kōtoku Shūsui, who had read Kropotkin and
had met with anarcho-syndicalists during a visit to the
United States. He was accused of treason and executed
a few years later. Japan harshly repressed anarchism and
anything else considered subversive, including liberalism
and socialism. Anarcho-communism emerged in Japan in
the late 1920s after an unsuccessful attempt by anarchists
to collaborate with the Bolshevik communists.

In Korea, huge numbers of anarchists fled the country
after the Japanese invaded in 1910. One Korean anarchist,
Shin Chaeho, wrote a manifesto in 1923 then joined the
Anarchist Federation of East Asia. He was arrested by the
Japanese in 1928, spent eight years in detention, and died
in prison. Korean anarchists succeeded in establishing a
liberated zone in Manchuria from 1929 to 1931.

One of the first anarchists in China was a woman
named He Zhen. She and her husband Liu Shipei moved
to Tokyo in 1904, where she started the first Chinese
anarchist journal, *Natural Justice*. They believed that anarchist ideas could be found in traditional Chinese culture,
especially peasant culture, but that anarchism could only
be achieved if the Chinese propensity for obedience could
be broken. Other Chinese anarchists were based in Paris,
where their focus was on the emancipation of women.
Their magazine *New Era* was quite intellectual and didn't
appeal to the masses.

Anarchism exercised a strong influence on the

revolutionary left in China in the 1920s, but the movement faltered in the 1930s as nationalist and communist
forces gained in strength. Chinese anarchists nevertheless continued to advocate a cultural revolution based
on education, the emancipation of women, and the pro-
motion of cosmopolitanism (rather than nationalism),
in part through the adoption of Esperanto. The goal, as
they saw it, was the liberation of the individual from old
habits of obedience. Some anarchists were also active in
anarcho-syndicalist organizations. When Mao's Communists seized power in 1949, some Chinese anarchists
went into exile in Hong Kong, Taiwan, and the United
States.

THOMAS: Let's not forget Africa. Some traditional societies have been described as "anarchist systems" because
of their horizontal political structure and an absence of
social classes.

FRANCIS: Indeed. Sam Mbah and I.E. Igariwey say in
their book *African Anarchism*:

> To a greater or lesser extent, all of these traditional Afri-
> can societies manifested 'anarchic elements' which upon
> close examination, lend credence to the historical truism
> that governments have not always existed. They are but
> a recent phenomenon and are, therefore, not inevitable
> in human society. While some 'anarchic' features of tra-
> ditional African societies existed largely in past stages
> of development, some of them persist and remain pro-
> nounced to this day.

THOMAS: Anarchist movements and revolutionary trade unions appeared in Africa in the late nineteenth century, especially in present-day South Africa, Mozambique, and Angola.

FRANCIS: I confess I don't know much about this part of anarchist history, so instead of spouting a lot of nonsense I'd rather not say any more.

THOMAS: You've been talking about anarchists who were active in struggles in different parts of the world. But there are other kinds of anarchists, aren't there—people who are anarchists at heart, who support the anarchist cause but never become militants or commit violent acts.

FRANCIS: Yes, there are intellectuals and artists who identify as anarchists in solidarity with the exploited masses, or who feel anarchy is the only ideological position in tune with the freedom to think and create. In the late nineteenth and early twentieth centuries, "individualist" anarchists advocated shortening the work day. They established communes called "free zones" where they could practice nudism, free love, and vegetarianism. In Portugal, they opposed bull-fighting, out of compassion for the bulls. These free zones embodied some of the spirit of Charles Fourier's idea of phalanstery, utopian communal housing arrangements that he proposed in the early nineteenth century, and which his followers later took to the United States. Free zones were incubators for new ideas, which were spread through newspapers. The zones also served as safe havens for revolutionaries on the run.

So you see, anarchism is more than just a social move-ment. It advances a cultural revolution, too. In the nine-teenth century, a moderate, liberal republican in France or the United States considered it perfectly normal and reasonable for a teacher to hit a student; for women to have fewer rights than men; for homosexuality to be labelled a disease and a crime; for people to work more than ten hours a day, six days a week; for military service to be compulsory; and for the state to impose the death penalty and colonize other people's lands. Anarchists thought otherwise. They extolled the benefits of equality between the sexes, co-education, free love, and a world without armies, war, and the death penalty. Anarchists were thrown in prison for distributing information about contraception and abortion.

Anarchism ran out of steam during the first half of the twentieth century, after the victories of the Marxist-Leninists in Russia and the Maoists in China. Some on the extreme left claimed that the Bolshevik victory proved the superiority of centralized state power over the anarchist idea of self-management without a state. The American anarchist Lucy Parsons, for example, joined the Com-munist Party in 1939. And yet it was anarchists who first denounced the lethal authoritarian drift of the USSR. And it was the Red Army that massacred the anarchist Black Army in the Ukraine, after the anarchists helped the Red Army defeat the reactionary White Army in the Russian Civil War. Reactionary forces also massacred anarchists in Germany and Spain. So part of the reason that anar-chist influence declined in the 1920s and '30s was simply because so many of them were murdered.

During the Second World War, German anarchists were among the first to be sent to concentration camps such as Dachau, along with communists and social democrats. Anarchists have always been persecuted, tortured, shot, and massacred during political struggles. And yet a number of anarchists fought in the armed resistance against the Nazis. By the end of the Second World War, and with the start of the Cold War between the Western liberal powers and the Soviet Union, anarchism was just a shadow of what it had been.

THOMAS: During a war such as the Second World War anarchy is not really an option, because the struggle is between states. The only way you can put anarchist principles into practice is by refusing to take part in the war, as a conscientious objector, draft dodger, or deserter. That was the path I chose in the 1950s. I refused to do my military service in France. It was compulsory at the time, lasted twenty-seven months, and included a tour of duty in Algeria during the war of independence. I had no desire to learn how to kill my fellow human beings, so I evaded the draft. Though military sentences are supposed to be irrevocable, France declared an amnesty several years later for those who made the choice I did. But it was too late for me; I had already severed my ties with France.

I arrived in Quebec in the early 1960s, at the start of the Quiet Revolution. (It was very quiet, indeed, and it's still not finished, because half a century later we're still debating the place of religious symbols in public.) I witnessed what might be seen as a kind of "mass anarchy": in a matter of years, the Québécois rejected the authority of the church. Then I witnessed, from a distance, that other mass anarchist movement, May '68, when the youth of France rejected all forms of authority. That was when I realized that radical change is possible in any society.

FRANCIS: Exactly. After the Second World War, anarchism reappeared in the West in the counter-culture movement, starting with the Provos in Amsterdam in 1965, then May '68 in France, and student movements in West Germany, the USA, and Quebec. Anarchists were critical not only of the state and capitalism, but also of mass consumerism and the bureaucratization of social relations. Anarchist ecologists such as Murray Bookchin were among the first to denounce pollution from a radical perspective, and even to raise the alarm about global warming. Anarchism is very supportive of the Third World, and anarchists supported anti-colonialist and anti-imperialist struggles in Algeria, Vietnam, and Cuba.

Several Cuban anarchists fought in the Cuban revolution, and were active in local trade unions. However, when Fidel Castro took power the Communist Party took control of the unions and other social organizations, and expelled the anarchists. Some decided to leave the country. Others remained to challenge the new regime and ended up in prison, where several died.

The Cuban anarchists published several texts denouncing the Castro regime as a dictatorship. However, one anarchist who stayed in Cuba, Manuel Gaona Sousa, betrayed his comrades. He persuaded other anarchists to sign a document denouncing the anti-Castro anarchists, claiming they were in the pay of the United States. Sousa also claimed there were no anarchists in Cuban prisons, and that money intended to help prisoners was being diverted into private pockets.

Nevertheless, the anti-Castro anarchists documented the treatment they received in Cuban prisons, which was even more brutal than what anarchists endured in other countries, such as Spain, France, and the United States. Two Cuban anarchists, Suria Linsuain and Carmelina Casanova, served only a few years of their thirty-year sentences for "counter-revolutionary" activities, but their prison conditions were so harsh that they died shortly after being released.

Anti-Castro anarchists in Cuba received support from some anarchist networks in North and South America, but in Europe the situation was more difficult. The Spanish anarchist Federica Montseny, living in exile in France, said: "It is not popular to attack Castro in Europe." Even Daniel Cohn-Bendit, one of the heroes of May '68, was wary of the Cuban anarchists, suspecting them of being in the pay of the US secret services. So did the Italian Anarchist Federation. It wasn't until the 1970s that the situation began to change.

In the '70s and '80s, in Western Europe and the USA, the extreme left was mostly Marxist-Leninist, adhering to the Soviet, Albanian, Maoist, or Trotskyist line. Anarchism was sidelined, though anarchists carried on discreetly. In the decades since, anarchism has captured the imagination of marginalized youth, counter-cultural movements such as punk, and activists in the alter-globalization movement.

Studies have shown that many anarchists are employed

and belong to unions, so today's anarchist is not necessarily marginalized, though obviously some are. In any case, unions no longer have the revolutionary importance they had a century ago. After the Second World War, unions abandoned revolutionary struggle, and anarchists know that if they speak out they will find little support within their unions.

In some countries such as France, where anarchist organizations have been around much longer, there are more older anarchists. This offers advantages (transmission of memory, permanence, stability) and disadvantages (a stranglehold on organizations by the old guard resulting in ideological and political rigidity). In other contexts, where organizations come and go quickly, activists tend to be much younger. In France, the Fédération anarchiste has been around since 1945 and has more than a hundred committees across the country, which explains why there are so many French anarchists over the age of fifty. The opposite is true in Quebec, where anarchist organizations are generally younger and more ephemeral. In other French anarchist networks, such as antifascist and squatter groups, there are fewer middle-aged activists. Let's face it, it's easier to be an anarchist when you're young and childless and without too many responsibilities. It's harder when you're in your thirties or forties, especially if you have children and want to provide a comfortable home life for them. The "system" exercises a powerful attraction, and not surprisingly many activists fall into line as they get older.

Streams of Anarchist Thought

THOMAS: Maybe we shouldn't try to classify anarchists by social class, since as you say there are anarchists in all social classes. Maybe it's better to categorize anarchists by the causes they support. An anarchist may be opposed to all forms of authority, but dedicate herself or himself to fighting one particular form of authority.

FRANCIS: I agree that's a more interesting approach, as long as we acknowledge that the boundaries between different streams or schools of anarchism are not always clear. That said, anarchists do have quite different ideas about politics and society, and what the priorities should be for activism. Here are six distinct streams of anarchist thought that we can look at: anarcho-communism, anarcho-syndicalism, insurrectionary anarchism, individualist anarchism, anarcha-feminism, and anarcho-ecology. But let me also say that what I've been doing from the start of our discussion is giving you *my* ideas about anarchism, based on my readings and *my* experience in certain anarchist networks. Talk to another anarchist and you'll get a different history of anarchism, and he or she will probably dispute some of my answers to your questions.

THOMAS: Well, I've always assumed you're answering my questions from your own perspective. So let's go on. I'd like to hear you talk about each of the streams you just mentioned, and the names associated with them, even if some of the streams are less popular these days. Let's start with anarcho-communism. The names that crop up are Bakunin and Kropotkin.

FRANCIS: Anarcho-communism advocates the reorganization of society around local communities, such as neighbourhoods, villages, or small administrative units (which in France are called *communes*, hence the idea of communism). Each unit would be self-governed by an autonomous, local assembly. "The people" become the agents of change, in the sense that they organize themselves and debate, discuss, and make collective decisions in local assemblies or other kinds of face-to-face meetings. The revolution happens when people take the initiative to organize themselves at the grassroots level, where they live.

The transformation to an anarchist society may be violent, if an armed struggle is necessary to expropriate land or seize apartment buildings. After the revolution, self-governing units or collectives can coordinate their efforts by federating, but each unit retains its autonomy: the federation cannot impose decisions on the local collectives. Some anarchists take inspiration from the Zapatista revolution in southern Mexico in 1994, which gave local peasant collectives the freedom to govern themselves through local assemblies.

THOMAS: For anarcho-syndicalism, the name that comes first to my mind is Michel Chartrand, the outspoken Quebec trade union leader.

FRANCIS: Anarcho-syndicalism sees unions as the fundamental unit of self-management and revolution. This stream of anarchism takes its inspiration from the struggles of workers, and is often associated with the writings of the French activists Émile Pouget and Fernand Pelloutier. Anarcho-syndicalists believe that the revolution begins in the workplace and is achieved through a general strike or armed struggle. The goal is to bring down the capitalist system, seize control of the means of production—the factories, mines, etc.—and self-manage them. Unions are seen as a way of bringing together in common cause groups of people that are often isolated from one another—women and men sex workers, for example, or consumers and the unemployed. They would work together to improve their conditions. Just as with anarcho-communism, society would be organized and the economy coordinated by federating unions within or across economic sectors. But the autonomy of the rank and file workers would be guaranteed. The federation would not be able to impose its will on local unions. Anarcho-communism and anarcho-syndicalism could be combined, because many anarcho-communists claim to be primarily focussed on the proletariat and the class struggle.

THOMAS: For insurrectionary anarchism, perhaps Louise Michel.

FRANCIS: Insurrectionary anarchism seeks direct confrontation with the state and its police. It's a tenacious, unyielding approach to anarchism. It's the approach taken by the Black Blocs. By confronting and fighting the police, anarchists hope to provoke mass insurrection and revolution. Either the skirmishes will inspire the population to join the insurrection, or the confrontation between police and protesters will be so harsh that the balance of power in society will shift, leading to a revolution. Even if nothing changes, rioting is still seen as worthwhile in itself because it opens an exciting space for freedom, allows people to express a radical critique through concrete action (by vandalizing a bank, for example), and offers the real political experience of confronting a real enemy, the police. You often see insurrectionary anarchism at anti-austerity protests, for example in Greece and Chile, and even in Quebec during the long student strike of 2012.

THOMAS: For individualist anarchism, I can't think of a representative figure.

FRANCIS: Individualist anarchism traces its roots to the nineteenth-century German philosopher Max Stirner. As the name suggests, it emphasizes individual freedom over social and ideological constraints. But it never loses sight of the ultimate goal, the emancipation and flowering of the collective, which is seen as necessary for the complete emancipation of the individual. This kind of anarchism attaches more importance to the liberation of the individual from all inhibitions, whether psychological, sexual, or artistic. It's closely associated with the French libertarian communes called "free zones" that I mentioned earlier, involving Victor Serge, Émile Armand, and others, around 1900. Some anarchists of this persuasion called themselves "individualists"; in France, they called themselves *en dehors* (outsiders).

Individualist anarchism is also associated with the illegal practice of "expropriating" money from the bourgeoisie. The Bonnot Gang was infamous for a spree of armed robberies in France and Belgium during the winter of 1911–12. They claimed to be anarchists redistributing the money through activist networks, and were sometimes given refuge in the French "free zones."

Some of the stories about these kinds of anarchists are quite extraordinary. For example, there was a group of Spanish anarchists in the 1920s who robbed banks to help finance the struggle against the dictatorship of Primo de Rivera. The group then sailed off to the Americas, where they continued their spree in the southern United States, Mexico, Cuba, Argentina, and Chile. They were eventually arrested in France in connection with a plot to assassinate King Alphonso XIII of Spain. The government of Argentina accused them of killing an Argentine policeman and demanded their extradition, but an international campaign of solidarity was organized; even liberals and socialists signed petitions in their support. The three anarchists were eventually freed and deported to Belgium. Among them was Buenaventura Durruti, who had been a member of Los Solidarios, an armed self-defence group that protected Spanish trade unionists from attacks by the authorities and the extreme right. Durruti was one of the anarchist heroes of the Spanish Civil War, in which he died.

Individualist anarchists, like insurrectionary anarchists, can be insolent and provocative, even towards other anarchists. They sometimes mock the seriousness and formality of general assemblies, and criticize the rhetoric of class struggle and revolutionary trade unionism, which they consider passé and stifling. The provocations are both a game and an ideological challenge.

Anarchism and Feminism

THOMAS: There's no shortage of anarcha-feminists. I think of Louise Michel, Séverine, Voltairine de Cleyre, and Emma Goldman.

FRANCIS: True, but it's important to note that many women anarchists refuse to call themselves feminists. They say feminism is a bourgeois movement associated with liberal demands such as the right to vote. For example, in Spain in the 1930s there was an anarchist organization called Mujeres Libres (Free Women). Only women were allowed to join. It had about thirty thousand members, but they didn't call themselves feminists. They published a newspaper that discussed issues affecting women: trade unionism, education, prostitution, love, marriage, and child-bearing. They even taught each other how to use guns.

Obviously, anarcha-feminism tries to bring together anarchism and feminism. The feminist part of the equation injects a critique of patriarchy and sexism into the heart of anarchist circles, where there is no shortage of male chauvinists and sexual aggressors, protected as often as not by their male comrades. Male solidarity comes first! But anarcha-feminism rejects, on principle, solutions coming from the state. It also tries to inject some anarchism into feminism. It's critical of the hierarchical structures of institutionalized feminist organizations. And it's not content to just change laws. It champions women's autonomy, individually and collectively.

There is an ongoing debate about which should take precedence, feminism or anarchism. Susan Brown, a Canadian feminist and anarchist, says that feminism is not necessarily anarchist, but anarchism must, *in principle*, be feminist:

> Feminism as a whole recognizes the iniquity of the oppression of women by men; anarchism opposes oppression of all kinds....As anarchism is a political philosophy that opposes *all* relationships of power, it is inherently feminist. An anarchist who supports male domination contradicts the implicit critique of power which is the fundamental principle upon which all of anarchism is built.

Other women, such as Lynne Farrow and Peggy Kornegger, disagree. They argue that, to be consistent, feminists must be anarchists, since the domination and exploitation that women have experienced should motivate them to abolish not just one system of domination, the patriarchy, but all systems of domination.

In this respect, modern anarcha-feminism is reviving ideas put forward a century ago by Voltairine de Cleyre and others, who saw women as a gender "class" dominated and exploited, as a class, by men. They also argued that heterosexual relationships are necessarily unequal and disadvantageous for women, when considered in the context of domestic chores, parental duties, and sexual equality. Similarly, modern anarcha-feminists critique heteronormality, reminding us of the importance of respecting (and practicing) sexual diversity.

Radical feminism, and the radical fringes of the lesbian, gay, bisexual, and transgender movement (LGBT; often called "queer") provide interesting examples of how to organize and act in an egalitarian and consensual manner. Radical feminists have experimented with different ways of facilitating discussion and decision-making in meetings. For example, they open and close meetings by going around the table, allowing everyone to say a few words about their state of mind, their expectations, and their grievances. This has two benefits: it helps others at the meeting to better understand why a particular person expresses herself the way she does, and it ensures that it's not always the same people who do most of the talking. They also change the meeting facilitator from time to time.

It can sometimes be difficult to distinguish the radical feminists from the anarcha-feminists. For example, in Quebec there's a collective called Les Sorcières (The Witches). It self-identifies as "radical feminist." It declares itself opposed to the patriarchy, the state, and capitalism. It functions in an autonomous and self-managed manner, without a hierarchy, and participates in a number of activities in the Quebec anarchist network.

THOMAS: And yet, when we think of anarchists we think of

men first. We seem to unconsciously accept that the patriarchal system will go on forever, that women have never
overthrown it and never will. We also seem to accept that
history is written by men, and remembers men above all.
Just look at Jean Préposiet's book, *Histoire de l'anarchisme*
(History of anarchism). Though published in 1993, it mentions Simone de Beauvoir only once, in connection with a
book by Céline, while Sartre is mentioned a dozen times.
Louise Michel is mentioned twice, once as a participant
in a convention bringing together thirty-odd anarchists,
and then in reference to a militant group named after her.
Emma Goldman is mentioned only once, as a signatory of
a manifesto written by thirty-three anarchists. And that's
it! It's as if all the other anarcha-feminists—the Mujeres
Libres of Spain, Voltairine de Cleyre, Lucy Parsons—
it's as if they never existed!

FRANCIS: That just goes to show that even anarchists
harbour sexist prejudices. And yet, women have been
there from the birth of anarchism and are still there today,
even where men least expect to find them. For example,
when we think of the Black Blocs or other stereotypes
of the anarchist, what immediately comes to mind is a
man; the media seem to always talk of anarchist vandals
as men. But I can tell you that in many cases, the vandals
are women. That's certainly the case in Germany. But it
was also true at the G20 summit in Toronto in 2010 and
during the Quebec student strike in 2012, where many
women took part in the Black Blocs. Sometimes, they
formed women-only affinity groups, for better solidarity
and communication. The presence of women in the Black

Blocs shatters stereotypes of femininity and masculinity, by proving that women can be in the thick of the action and even resort to violence while still showing concern for others. Activists report that women-only affinity groups tend to care for each other, whereas men in the Black Blocs tend to act as "lone wolves." This shows that characteristics traditionally identified as masculine and feminine—aggression and concern for others—are in fact asexual and can coexist and find expression in the same person, regardless of sex.

Many feminists, including Susan Brown and Andrea Dworkin, have pointed out that the otherwise progressive, radical men who participated in the New Left in the 1960s never took women seriously, let alone feminists. Even today, some anarchist groups are controlled by men and resist feminism. Obviously, this varies from group to group and country to country. In Quebec, there are more and more women in anarchist groups, and they are sometimes the majority, exercising a strong influence. But it's still common to see tasks divided on the basis of sex, with men doing the more prestigious tasks that give them greater influence, such as writing texts, planning actions, giving speeches and talking to the media. Women are too often left doing essential but less prestigious tasks: taking minutes, setting up and cleaning meeting rooms, preparing meals.

It's discouraging, but not that surprising. Even if male anarchists affirm in principle the political importance of autonomy, some take offence when feminists want to meet on their own, without men, to discuss their political problems and collectively seek solutions. Anarchists know that it's often better to meet on their own, not with socialists, communists, employers, or the police. But faced with feminists, anarchist men claim to be excluded, saying that women are practicing reverse sexism and are anti-men.

Let me give you an example from my own experience that may seem absurd, but nonetheless exposes this bad faith for what it is. In 2003 I took part in protests against the G8 summit in France. I stayed in a temporary, self-governing encampment of about four thousand anarchists called Village alternatif, anticapitaliste et antiguerre (Alternative, anti-capitalist, anti-war village). Staying there was one of the most interesting anarchist experiences of my life. Right next door was another, smaller encampment for women only, called the G-Spot. A few dozen feminists were staying there. Some men couldn't resist entering the women's encampment. They urinated in the encampment, argued with the women, pushed them around, and even slapped and punched them. At the wrap-up meeting for the village, one man had the audacity to rant about the G-Spot, claiming it had unjustly excluded men and contravened the anarchist ideal of equality.

In activist couples, it's usually the woman who does more of the domestic and parenting work. More often than not, the woman is seen as the partner of the man. If they separate, she's usually the one to leave the activist group, later to be replaced by the man's new partner.

There are many documented cases of sexual harassment, domestic violence, and sexual assault committed by anarchist men. Anarchists are quick to defend the victims of violence when it's perpetrated by dominant powers, and you'd think they'd be just as quick to denounce male violence against women. But when the aggressor is a comrade, especially an experienced militant with many friends in the movement, suddenly the equivocation and the counter-accusations begin. The victim's claims are minimized or rejected ("it wasn't that serious," or "she's a liar"), or she's blamed for the attack ("she was drunk," or "she didn't clearly say 'no'"), or she's accused of stirring up internal trouble and weakening the group. The other men in the group risk being ostracized if they break male solidarity and side with the woman: they're no longer invited to protest or party with their former comrades. For all these reasons, it's easier not to admit that male violence against women is every bit as systemic as racist violence or police brutality. You might think I'm exaggerating, but I've heard many stories during my years of activism in anarchist networks in Quebec and France.

Though it happens much less often, there are also cases of militant lesbian anarchists harassing and assaulting other women anarchists. It's particularly troubling when it's an experienced activist taking advantage of her prestige to pressure a newcomer. The experienced activist claims to understand feminism, and support the principle of "no means no" when it's between a man and a woman, but then she turns around and harasses or sexually assaults another woman.

It all just goes to show that anarchist networks don't operate outside society and are just as prone to systems of domination. Just like republicans, liberals, or even Catholics, anarchists are a long way from putting their beautiful principles into practice when it comes to relations between men and women, both in public and in private.

THOMAS: These kinds of sexist attitudes are everywhere in patriarchal societies, so it's not surprising to see them even among men dedicated to noble causes like erasing the gap between rich and poor. Equality between men is assumed in progressive circles, but the same cannot be said of equality between men and women. Being an anarchist doesn't necessarily make you less sexist.

There are many examples of this hypocrisy. During the Spanish Civil War, libertarian organizations preached equality between the sexes, but women couldn't make themselves heard in mixed groups. They were reduced to sewing clothes and caring for the sick, and obviously needed an organization of their own to defend themselves and to make their voices heard. That's what gave rise to Mujeres Libres.

The same thing happened in the United States in the Black Power movement. In a 1968 article titled "Poor Black Woman," Patricia Robinson draws a parallel between male domination and capitalism. The black woman, she says, "allies herself with the have-nots in the wider world and their revolutionary struggle." The Black Panthers, who fought to defend the civil rights of black Americans, were profoundly sexist. In an addendum to its rules, the party stated, "Do not take liberties with women," which shows that the rules were intended solely for men.

FRANCIS: Yes, the Black Panthers are a good example of men who were revolutionary but sexist. African-American women activists denounced them. And women anarchists are still organizing their own networks in the face of sexism. Éloise Gaudreau, an activist with the Quebec revolutionary group L'Union communiste libertaire, says this logical contradiction between revolution and sexism surfaces mostly as political tension. The women anarchists she talked to helped her to understand that while anarchist groups are not completely egalitarian, they are more egalitarian than other activist groups, such as student unions. There is always a tension between the demands and criticisms of women who are trying to expand equality within a group and the more or less overt resistance of the men.

Sometimes in the struggle for equality women find they must withdraw for a time into women-only groups in order to protect themselves, to help one another, to collectively reflect, and to develop their own analyses and tactics without having to justify and explain themselves to men. All dominated, subordinate groups do this at times, creating spaces where it is possible to meet separately from those who dominate them.

Hence the importance of anarcha-feminists, who are critiquing and contesting the patriarchy and male chauvinism in society in general, but also and especially within activist networks. It's a thankless task. The women continually have to remind us that "the private is political." They struggle with these issues in their own private lives. And they are often seen as troublemakers when they confront problems that the group would rather ignore. When women accuse male comrades of sexual harassment or assault, they're often asked to leave the group, or they're expelled outright. They lose comrades, friends, and relationships. But does the blame for all this lie with the feminists, or with misogynist men and aggressors?

Anarcho-Ecology

THOMAS: The last kind of anarchism I want to hear you talk about is anarcho-ecology, which makes me think of groups like Greenpeace and activists like José Bové.

FRANCIS: Anarcho-ecology criticizes capitalism for its destructive impact on animals, human beings, and the environment. It's anti-speciesist, meaning that it refuses to distinguish and discriminate among species. Its activists are often vegetarian or vegan, and sometimes take action against pharmaceutical companies that test their products on animals. Of all the various schools of anarchism, anarcho-ecology is probably the most critical of contemporary society, and the most alarmist.

There are three sub-currents of anarcho-ecology. Primitivism is the most radical, and the one most often caricatured. According to the primitivists, humanity was at its best during the paleolithic age. Its chief proponent is John Zerzan, a writer in Oregon who rejects the alienating effects of civilization. For Zerzan, that includes language, numbers, technology, and even the calculation of time. He says these established systems come between us and the world, alienating us from reality without our being aware of it. He points to common expressions that we use without thinking: "I have no time" or "I'm running out of time."

The second sub-current is "deep ecology." It's associated with militant groups such as Earth First! and its offshoot, Earth Liberation Front. Authorities in the United States have called these activists "ecoterrorists" because they have freed animals from pharmaceutical company labs, set fire to construction projects and cars, and sabotaged logging machinery. Deep ecology preaches biological egalitarianism. It says that all living species are interdependent, that no one species has the right to consider itself superior to the others, and that biological diversity is essential for species to fully realize their potential. Seen in this light, the human species is neither at the summit nor the centre, it's just one species among all the others. Deep ecology denounces industrial agriculture, on the grounds that it dominates and exploits nature for the benefit of humans.

The third sub-current of anarcho-ecology is called "libertarian municipalism." It was developed by Murray Bookchin, an American writer who proposed reorganizing society around local citizens' assemblies, which could better take into account regional ecology.

Well, that gives you some idea of the main schools of anarchist thought. But there are many others. There are anti-fascist anarchists. There's queer anarchism, which is related to radical feminism but expands the critique of domination to include all forms of sexual identity and practice. And there's post-colonial anarchism, which focuses on the struggles of the First Nations of the Americas and migrant communities, all of whom are victims of racism.

The Black Flag and the Circle-A

THOMAS: The different schools of anarchism that we've been talking about all band together under the black flag, the symbol of anarchism. But I see that each school also has its own colours.

FRANCIS: No one really knows where the black flag comes from. Some say the idea comes from the pirate flag. Others claim Louise Michel was the first to wave a black flag during the Paris Commune. Since some anarchists also support communism (without the state), anarcho-communists and anarcho-syndicalists sometimes fly a flag that is half black, half red. Anarcha-feminists carry a black and purple flag, anarcho-ecologists a green and black one. Some queer anarchists use the anarcha-feminist flag; others wave a black and pink flag, or a flag that is half black and half the rainbow colours of the LGBT community.

The letter A inside a circle, called the circle-A, is another symbol of anarchism. A group called Jeunes libertaires (Libertarian Youth) claimed to have invented it in Paris in 1964, though some say it was already in use in the late nineteenth century. The Jeunes libertaires were looking for a symbol that was easy to paint on the walls of the Paris metro, to counter the slogans of an extreme right-wing group called Jeune nation (Young Nation), which supported France's war in Algeria.

I heard that directly from one of the Jeunes libertaires, a woman named Helyette Bess. She provided illegal abortions in France in the 1950s and '60s. She later became a member of the Féderation anarchiste and the French revolutionary group Action directe. She also started a library and information centre in Paris called Jargon libre (Free jargon).

Internal Debates

FRANCIS: Anarchists generally support mergers and alliances between different groups and schools of thought. They try to arrive at a synthesis of positions through consensus, while allowing each group the right of veto in case of a fundamental disagreement. This synthesist approach is based in the belief that diversity is stronger than homogeneity.

But not all anarchists agree. Some argue that too much diversity undermines anarchism's strength. They prefer to mobilize all anarchists under the banner of a single, grand cause, usually the anti-capitalist class struggle. That was the position taken by Nestor Makhno, a Ukrainian anarchist, after the massacre of the Black Army by the Red Army in the 1920s. Makhno urged all anarchists to unite and adopt a common platform, decided by the majority. Anarchists should respect this common platform, he argued, even if there are fundamental disagreements, because unity is stronger than diversity.

A third approach contends that rants, arguments, and heated debates serve a positive purpose: they help sort good ideas from bad ideas, as well as good anarchists from bad anarchists. This is the approach taken by insurrectionary anarchists and individualists.

In the real world, the differences between various schools of anarchism are not always clear. Individuals and groups can belong to more than one school, and sometimes identifying with a particular school can lead to breaks in alliances and friendships. There are conflicts between anarcho-syndicalists and primitivists, and between anarcha-feminists and anarcho-communists or insurrectionists.

For example, in the early twentieth century, anarchist publications usually supported anarcho-syndicalism, while distancing themselves from those who practiced what's often called "expropriation," robbing and making counterfeit money to fund anarchist groups. In Argentina, the anarcho-syndicalist newspaper *La Protesta* condemned robbery, claiming it was dishonourable and risked alienating honest workers who might otherwise be drawn to anarchism. But another anarchist newspaper, *La Antorcha*, supported the "expropriators," arguing that under capitalism, "since it has been demonstrated that property is theft, the only robbers in these parts are the property owners."

THOMAS: The idea that "property is theft" probably comes from Proudhon's influential book, *What is Property? An Inquiry Into the Principle of Right and of Government.*

FRANCIS: Louise Michel also made that point. She saw capitalists as vampires feeding on the labour of others. Her book *Prise de possession* (Taking possession) calls for "the end of theft eternally committed by the privileged and stupidly accepted by the masses."

Other issues have divided anarchists at various times. Prostitution is the subject of intense debate these days. Feminists have several conflicting positions: prohibitionists call for an outright ban on prostitution and prostitutes; abolitionists want to end the profession by helping prostitutes leave it and penalizing those who benefit from it, i.e., the pimps and clients; regulators advocate decriminalizing and regulating prostitution, while anti-regulators advocate decriminalization without regulation.

This division is reflected in the intense debate among anarchists. Some anarchists support sex workers, and help them form autonomous organizations to defend their rights, their interests, and their dignity. That's the anarcho-syndicalist approach. Other anarchists consider prostitution to be one of the most revolting forms of exploitation. They point out that when anarchists talk about "free love" they're not using the word *free* in the same way that liberals do, namely the freedom to buy and sell anything, even your body. They argue that, like friendship, "free love" must be without any exchange of money in order to be truly free, and no one should have to sell themselves for money. But they also recognize that people in financial difficulty sometimes decide to prostitute themselves. These anarchists call for solidarity with prostitutes, not criminalization. Prostitution may be "just another job" but it is never emancipatory. In a liberal "free market," all work is a form of exploitation, and prostitution is no exception. Some jobs are more difficult than others, but prostitution is one of the most difficult and the most dangerous—there is a risk of violence, disease, and serious psychological harm.

Ultimately, the decision to prostitute oneself seems to be largely determined by structural social factors, which explains why, in the overwhelming majority of cases, it's women who sell their bodies and men who buy them—with the women often coming from disadvantaged classes and groups suffering racial discrimination. In Canada, for example, the poorest women who suffer the most racial discrimination, such as First Nations women, find themselves in the most miserable and dangerous situations as prostitutes. Seen in that light, anarchists and feminists hope that women and men can free themselves from sex work, which is rooted in patriarchy, capitalism, and racism. But how best to address the problem is the question.

In 2012 the Quebec radical feminist collective Les Sorcières (The Witches) published an editorial in their newspaper explaining their position on sexual exploitation. It said, "the question is full of risks, because we know that whatever position we take in public will lead to debate, conflict, personal attacks, and even breakdowns in friendships." While hoping for the eventual disappearance of prostitution, the collective acknowledged that "the sex industry will only collapse when we abolish the patriarchy, capitalism, and racism." While waiting for that day, the editorial argued, it was important to remember that "all women are concerned about the sex industry," to remain in solidarity with sex workers, to denounce police brutality against prostitutes, to listen to those "who speak out about what they have lived," and to help women "who want to get out of prostitution [to do so] as easily as possible." The position expressed by Les Sorcières was thus abolitionist, anarchist, and in solidarity.

Anarchists come in all shapes and sizes. Some anarchists adhere to a particular school of thought; others don't follow any school or may belong to groups or movements that don't call themselves anarchist but nonetheless operate on anarchist principles and fight racism, war, or police brutality. Some anarchists are active in collectives that prepare and distribute free food, such as the network

Food Not Bombs. Others, such as Anarchist Black Cross, support revolutionary political prisoners by visiting them in prison and providing them with financial support and political literature. In the early twentieth century, groups such as the Committee for the Defence of Social Prisoners and Deportees, in Argentina, even tried to organize prison escapes.

What Makes a Real Anarchist?

THOMAS: If I'm understanding all this correctly, anarchism is the theory, anarchy is the practice, and an anarchist is someone who practices anarchy. But so far we've restricted our definition of anarchy to its historical meaning: the absence of a state, a leader, a hierarchy, and power. After hearing about the different schools of anarchism, I wonder if we need to expand our definition of anarchy to include people who criticize and challenge any form of authority that victimizes people or limits freedom and equality. Doing so would suggest that as soon as you criticize power (whether it's the state, the church, employers, money, the patriarchy, etc.) you become an anarchist. But is that true? Or is there a distinction to be made between a full-time, 24/7 anarchist fighting all forms of authority, someone we might call a pure anarchist, and, say, an anarcha-feminist, someone who's only part anarchist? To put it another way, is someone who fights against only one form of authority a real anarchist, if he or she accepts all the other forms of authority?

FRANCIS: Some people challenge specific forms of power—the state, capitalism, the patriarchy, whatever. Rather than try to label them anarchists, maybe it's better to just call them radical feminists, anti-capitalists, ecologists, etc. That doesn't mean some of them aren't organizing or acting in an anarchist way, or that anarchists can't learn from their examples and experiences. Of course, it's also true that republicans or liberals can be opposed to racism or sexism.

THOMAS: Another question, then, and this one has been bothering me from the start: why do anarchists want to destroy power, hierarchy, and authority? It can't be just for the sake of destruction, otherwise they'd be nihilists, not anarchists. There are so many different forms and degrees of anarchy. Some people are proactive, it seems to me, driven to destroy whatever authority is in power. Others seem to just get swept up in events, for example when a king dies with no immediate successor. And then there are people who, rather than fight authority, choose to ignore it completely and withdraw from an oppressive society. The most beautiful example, I think, is David Thoreau, who severed all ties with society, refusing to allow it any further authority over him.

FRANCIS: Yes, and there are also the examples of the "free zones" and the "outsiders," that I mentioned earlier.

THOMAS: In extreme situations, there are even people who, unable to destroy an authority, destroy themselves. It's their way of demonstrating to the world that the form of authority they're living under is intolerable. I'm thinking of the Buddhist monks who set themselves on fire in public during the Vietnam War.

So let me ask you again: Why do anarchists want to destroy power, hierarchy, and authority? Is it to substitute a freer and more egalitarian system?

FRANCIS: I'm going to toss the question back to you. After all, you've seen many powers and hierarchies at work. You were born in Paris in the 1930s, so you survived the Nazi occupation. Then you refused to do your military service in the French army, because that would have meant obeying an order to kill your fellow human beings in Algeria. You chose instead to come to Quebec, where you started out teaching in a private college run by the Catholic clergy. You were here during the October Crisis of 1970 when the Canadian government imposed the War Measures Act and rounded up hundreds of innocent people. You've held positions of authority as a teacher, a publisher, and a director of the Salon du livre de Montréal. Your life has been full of authority and hierarchies. What conclusions do you draw from all those experiences? Do you believe that freedom and equality are more dangerous and harmful than authority and hierarchies? Do you think there are any good reasons for fighting authority and hierarchies?

THOMAS: That's true, I grew up during the occupation. I had to hide with my family to escape the Nazis and the police. And after the war, when I was older, I lived in a patriarchal and misogynist society where military service was obligatory. So I have a "natural" instinct to reject all forms of authority and its representatives.

FRANCIS: So you're a kind of existential anarchist.

THOMAS: Is that what it's called? Well, it's also true that I've held positions of power in my life. But I hope I learned from my childhood experiences and didn't abuse my authority. Though I suppose you'd have to ask my colleagues and employees whether that was the case!

FRANCIS: Indeed!

THOMAS: But I keep coming back to *authority* and *power*. Which is the key word? By *power* I mean legal or de facto power over someone or something. It seems to me that authority is only detrimental if it's abusive, if it creates inequalities, if the person with authority forces people to do things that hinder their freedom.

FRANCIS: Are there any lawful authorities that don't create inequality? By definition, inequality exists whenever there is authority and hierarchy. Can you think of *any* enlightened, benevolent authorities? Or, to put it in your terms, is there any authority that doesn't exercise power?

As I said earlier, some anarchists believe that everyone has within themselves the potential to be dominant and the potential not to be dominant. Which tendency prevails depends on the structure or the social system. Put someone in a position of authority and there's a good chance he or she will abuse their power, even if they think they're doing good.

Obviously, the power you exercised as a publisher or as director of the Salon du livre can't be compared to the Nazi dictatorship or the power of the French colonial army. But even if you were a good boss (which is for your employees to judge), anarchists would still argue that all hierarchical structures distort human relations. People in a position of authority inevitably attribute more importance to their own ideas and words than they do to the ideas, words, and even the needs and interests, of their subordinates. We instinctively act in ways, including deference and outright lying, that meet the needs of our superiors, because we know that our superiors have the power to reward and punish.

I'm no different. My position as a university professor affects my relations with the students and the secretaries, not to mention the janitors and the women who serve food in the cafeteria. I see the effect, too, when people in the street recognize me as an author or someone they've seen on TV talking to the media. It's impossible for me to have frank, honest, and equal relations with people in these situations. My position as a professor, with all the resources and benefits that provides, including public platforms to speak and make myself seen, enhances my stature and lends weight to my words.

Sometimes I'm at a punk rock concert, maybe one attended by lots of anarchists. It's late at night, and young people recognize me. They address me formally, using *vous*. They call me *monsieur* and ask if I'm going to give a particular course next semester. Even weirder, they thank me for supporting a particular cause, as if I'm doing them a favour! There's no malicious intent on their part, it just goes to show how human relations are distorted by differences in status and by relationships based on inequality. People thank me in the street during demonstrations, a political space where, in principle, everyone should be equal. Even if I try not to let it go to my head, my career choice entangles me in a hierarchy. So you see, it's authority that creates hierarchical social structures, and they're toxic. Hierarchies distort social relations and create inequalities and injustices. Workers get exploited, and deference leads to hypocrisy.

THOMAS: That's a pessimistic view of the world, though perhaps it's realistic, especially in the workplace. But take any two people at random, and isn't it true that one will always be superior to the other, socially, intellectually, physically, financially, etc.?

FRANCIS: Anarchists know only too well that some people have better skills than others. The cobbler is much better at fixing shoes than I am (to be honest, I don't know a thing about it, for all my fancy diplomas). The cardiologist can save my life. If it weren't for electricians, I'd freeze to death in Montreal in winter. There are so many trades and essential jobs that don't come with any authority or privilege. Without garbage collectors life in our cities would quickly become unbearable, and we'd risk dying in an epidemic. Yet garbage collectors enjoy no prestige and their salaries are low compared to doctors.

But think about the high-prestige experts for a

moment. Just because they have specialist knowledge, do we necessarily have to accept their authority? Bakunin says that four conditions must be in place to prevent the authority that arises from specialist knowledge from becoming illegitimate power, and dominant. The first two conditions forestall a monopoly of expertise: first, that no expertise or specialization be reserved for a single category of individuals (men, for example); second, that we should always try to consult other experts, whenever possible. The last two conditions highlight the importance of not confusing authority with power: that we be free to accept or reject the advice of experts; and that we be able to criticize them freely. As Bakunin says: "I bow before the authority of special men because it is imposed on me by my own reason."

Nor do there have to be hierarchies of assets, like property, if anarchist communism is practiced. Assets can be shared or pooled. Take, for example, the Montreal Anarchist Bookfair, which has been running every year since 2000. The anarchist collective that organizes it is egalitarian and self-managed. There is no director, no president, and no secretary, unlike the Salon du livre that you directed for years. The Montreal publishing house Lux Éditeur is another good example: it's a self-managed collective. Decisions are made by consensus, whenever possible. There is no director or secretary. Tasks are allocated according to the skills of the members.

Now, obviously, you could say, "But those organizations aren't perfect!" You could point to things that don't always run smoothly at the anarchist book fair or in Lux's office. You could remind me that only a few thousand

visitors attend the anarchist book fair, compared with
more than 100,000 at the Salon du livre. But that's the
trap that's always set for anarchists, highlighting a single
problem to demonstrate that all anarchist theory is unre-
alistic. "Wait, wait," the critics say. "There's a problem
here, with your theory and your high principles. Anarchy
may be a beautiful utopia, but it doesn't work in practice."
As if there aren't countless examples of problems and failures with authoritarian systems, including the state and
capitalism. If a few examples of failure were all it took to
reject a political or economic system, none would survive.
We'd have to reject liberalism. And yet it carries on very
well, doesn't it? If you're looking for a system that runs
without a hitch, you'll never find it.

When I talk about anarchy, people are always asking
me to explain how it would work on a global scale, or even
in a single country. They seem to think the question alone
is enough to show that anarchy is impossible and unrealis-
tic. The question is rhetorical, thrown in my face without
any serious thought given to the actual potential of anarchy. Anarchists know that in the current political context
we're a long way from being able to establish anarchy in
any country, let alone the whole world. So the question is
almost superfluous. But no one system has ever covered all
of humanity—not monarchy, or feudalism, or liberalism.
Capitalism may seem to be everywhere today, but work
is being done outside the market economy; think of the
immense amount of free labour done by women, and the
use of child labour and slave labour in some places.

Putting aside for a moment the debate over whether
we're in the end stages of capitalism, we seem stuck on

the idea that we need an enlightened leader or a benevolent elite to govern the planet and tell us what to do.
Because obviously, so the argument goes, ordinary people
like cobblers and nurses aren't capable of running the
world. Anarchy offers an alternative. It starts with basic
democracy: people meeting locally to discuss and decide
their common affairs. The next step is coordinating or
networking regionally, based on the principle of federal-
ism. Each local community would communicate its pref-
erences and decisions to the federation, but the federation
cannot impose its will on local communities. The system
wouldn't be without its flaws, but what system is perfect?
What system consistently puts its fundamental principles
into practice?

THOMAS: What is a "perfect system," for you? Is it one
run by direct democracy, based on principles of solidarity,
mutual assistance, and individual freedom?

FRANCIS: I'd rather say that all political systems are
imperfect and all political systems are inconsistent, at least
some of the time, in applying their principles and theories.
But people would rather point out the problems associated
with anarchism than seriously consider the possibility of
achieving anarchy. I think that's because many people find
the idea of living in an egalitarian, self-managed community too strange to contemplate: it's not the model we
grew up with in our families and schools; it's not what we
experience at work or playing team sports. When we read
novels or watch TV or movies, we almost never see examples of egalitarian collectives practicing self-management.

Instead, we're bombarded with images of heads of state
and police officers. There are endless TV series, big budget
films, and crime novels glorifying the police. How many
times do we have to watch stories about retired, off-duty,
or young police officers leaping into action to save their
families, their cities, or all of humanity? There are doc-
umentaries about the history and exploits of the police,
and reality TV shows about the police on patrol. I don't
think there's any other job that gets so much air time in
our culture as that of police officer. Is it any surprise then
that we're incapable of imagining a world without police?
Western culture glorifies the idea of a single authority
holding power. Not only is that considered the most effi-
cient way to run things, but we even claim it's the natural
way for human beings to live.

Power (Part II)

THOMAS: You've talked a lot about authority, but are
authority and power always synonymous?

FRANCIS: Generally, anarchists think of power, authority,
and domination as synonymous, as do many people. But
some anarchists, particularly those strongly influenced by
feminism, make further distinctions when they talk about
power. They're opposed to "power over," that is, the
power exercised by A over B. (A and B can be individuals,
groups, or classes.) "Power over" allows A to impose its
will on B, to force B to do something or to prevent B from

doing something. But they also talk about "power of," meaning the power of action, of doing something without exercising "power over" other people. "Power of" means the freedom and capacity to think and act, individually and collectively.

For anarchists, what's important is to fight "power over," the kind that dominates and constrains, and to promote "power of," the freedom and capacity to act. What distinguishes anarchist communism from state communism of the Marxist-Leninist kind is not just who controls the resources and the means of production, but who has power itself. Anarchist communism is "power with." It's "power of" in combination with other people, the power to act in common. We have so much more power to act and accomplish things when we develop our power in cooperation with others.

THOMAS: Going back to our initial definition of anarchy as absence of government, Jacques Attali has something interesting to say in his book *Demain, qui gouvernera le monde?* (Tomorrow, who will govern the world?). He writes, "for as long as man has thought, he has asked himself who controls the world. First he imagined that the gods governed nature, and there was nothing he could do. Then individual men, priests, soldiers, and oligarchs, set out to govern parts of the world and its peoples, and then the whole world. They are doing their best to conquer it all, with religious faith, with power. And with the market." Where do things stand now? There is every reason to believe that the world today is largely controlled by the United States and the market, as Howard Zinn shows in

his book *A People's History of the United States*. Zinn writes
about the foreign policy of a country that has more than
seven hundred military bases around the world, a country
that has intervened, directly or indirectly, in many other
countries, claiming to be defending democracy but in
fact protecting its own economic interests. As the nineteenth-century French fabulist Jean de La Fontaine said:
"The reason of those best able to have their way is always
the best."

Attali goes on to ask what the future holds.

Which country, coalition, or international organization
will be able to deal with the ecological, nuclear, economic, financial, social, political, and military threats to
the world? Which will be able to nurture and develop
the tremendous potential of the world's many cultures?
Should we give power over the world to religions? To
empires? To markets? Or do we give it back to individual
nations, retreating behind their closed borders?

Attali ends on a more optimistic note: "One day,
humanity will understand that it has everything to gain
by uniting around a democratic world government." But
couldn't we replace Attali's "democratic government"
with "anarchist society"? That way we could all be a little
bit anarchist and a little more optimistic.

In fact, I think we're all a little bit anarchist, throughout our lives. First, none of us are born equal, physically
or socially. Shirley Chisholm, who campaigned unsuccessfully to become the Democratic Party's presidential
nominee in the United States in 1972, said: "I've had to
fight doubly hard and of the two handicaps being black is

much less a drawback than being a woman." Inequalities follow us all our lives. We're also born at the mercy of our parents. We're dominated by them in our childhood. We leave the family home when we're considered adult enough to accept being dominated by others, or when we've learned to dominate others ourselves.

FRANCIS: I don't understand why you say that we are all "a little bit anarchist."

THOMAS: Because everyone without exception has to submit to someone or something representing an authority, and because human nature being what it is (or what I think it is), we all want to rid ourselves of that authority. Look at my own life. My mother was a practicing Jew and my father was a believer, though more out of habit than anything else. All through my youth I had to submit to their taboos: better not to make friends with non-Jews; don't date non-Jewish girls; and forget about a mixed marriage. Add to that what we suffered during the Second World War, and maybe you can understand why I always have this feeling of being in permanent revolt, even if it doesn't erupt into the open.

And don't forget, military service was compulsory in France when I was young. My call-up came when I was doing an internship in Quebec. I decided not to return. That made me a draft dodger, liable to imprisonment if I stepped foot in France. And that decision led me to a mixed marriage. So, as a young man, I contravened three forms of authority: parental, religious, and state.

FRANCIS: Yes, but you can rebel against an authority figure without being an anarchist. Your rebellion seems to have been more of a one-off protest. You didn't question the foundations of authority or challenge an entire system of domination.

THOMAS: Earlier we talked about different forms of control, or authority. I'd like to go back now and see if they truly are different, or are essentially the same. Off the top of my head I can think of at least six forms of authority (or power): parental authority, state authority, religious authority, the patriarchy, employers, and money. Are there others, such as the media? Can we look at each in turn, and see how anarchists respond to them?

FRANCIS: You've forgotten racism, but we can come back to that later. As for employers and money, both are part of capitalism. But before we look at forms of authority separately, I want to mention another way of looking at all this. Patricia Hill Collins and other feminists, especially African-American feminists, have developed the notion of overlapping systems of domination and oppression. Collins calls it "the matrix of domination." Each system has its institutions and each individual finds herself or himself at the intersection of several systems. It's called the theory of "intersectionality."

In my case, I'm one of the privileged, because I'm a middle-aged, heterosexual man, I receive a substantial salary as a university professor, and I have beige skin (which we insist on calling white to enhance the impression of purity). I'm at the intersection of several systems of domination, but I'm always in the upper stratum. You can analyze my life using these ideas about the matrix of domination and intersectionality, but where they are especially helpful is in understanding the lives of people who are stuck in lower social strata.

For example, the reality of a poor African-American woman in the United States cannot be understood by looking at her only as a woman, or only as an African-American, or only as poor. That's because these systems reinforce each other. The effects, however, are not simply cumulative. An African-American man in the United States is almost certain to be stopped and searched by the police at least once in his life, for no other reason than the colour of his skin. The chances increase if he is poor, but wealth alone does not protect him from racial profiling by the police. At best, an African-American with money can hire a good lawyer to get him out of a tight spot, whereas a poor African-American will quickly end up behind bars. Now, even if women are generally more disadvantaged than men, women are at lower risk of being stopped by the police. But if it does happen, a woman may pay twice: once by being arrested in the first place, and then again by being subjected to lewd comments if not sexual harassment.

The matrix of domination and intersectionality is complex, and it's not always easy to unravel the systems that entangle someone at a lower stratum. It's easier to examine each system of domination separately, at least to start, when we're looking at concrete cases of domination.

Parents and Children

THOMAS: In the course of a lifetime, each of us encounters many forms of authority. Parental authority, first, then the authority of the state, which affects everyone. Then there's religious authority, if one is born into a religious family or has faith, and the authority of the boss and money in the capitalist system.

FRANCIS: Well, you're in a better position to talk about parental authority, because you've been both a child and a father. You've endured the authority of your parents, and you've exercised parental authority over my sister and I, an authority that was given to you by the state. You also had to fend off challenges to your authority during our adolescent crises.

THOMAS: Parental authority is the first form of authority we submit to. We free ourselves from it gradually, and naturally, though each person does that differently depending on his or her circumstances, how they were brought up and educated, etc. I grew up in France, where the law says: "Parental authority is a cluster of rights and duties whose finality is the interest of the child." The father and mother have authority over the child until it legally becomes an adult, or until the state removes the child from the parental home to protect it or to ensure its health, morals, education, and development. So parents have a duty to help their children develop to the point where the child can make its own decisions and stand on its own two feet.

That's what your mother and I tried to do, as best we could. I tried not to bring you up the way my parents brought me up. When I was a child, most parents wanted their children to follow in their footsteps and perpetuate the family traditions, in terms of career, religion, and social circle. My parents wanted me to be an engineer, like my cousins. My mother wanted me to be a good Jew and marry a Jew. Instead I became a publisher and an atheist, and I married a non-Jew.

FRANCIS: Anarchists try to make relations between children and adults more egalitarian, and to encourage children to be free. But that's not easy to do when adults are themselves controlled by a political and economic system that imposes a work schedule on them, in turn forcing the adults to impose a schedule on their children. The children have to eat and go to bed at a certain time because the parents have to get up at a certain time to go to work. What's more, some liberal societies still allow adults to inflict corporal punishment on children. For anarchists, in the best of all possible worlds, children would be raised collectively and wouldn't be treated as the property of their biological or legal parents. The same principles also shape the way anarchists think about school.

THOMAS: The education I received in France was secular, from kindergarten to the end of high school. But the teacher's word was considered the absolute truth (not that that stopped me from questioning it). The only time we were encouraged to reflect upon the education system itself was in our *baccalauréat* exams, at the end of high school. We had to write an essay on Montaigne's famous maxim: "J'aime mieux une tête bien faite qu'une tête bien pleine." (A well-trained mind is better than a stuffed one.) Ironically, our essays were corrected by teachers who had themselves come up through a system that insisted the best way to educate young minds was to stuff them full of facts.

Obviously that's not the kind of education anarchists advocate. From what I understand, anarchists see traditional schooling as a means of reproducing and perpetuating the social structures of domination and exploitation. Anarchists prefer a libertarian system of education.

There are examples of schools that have tried to foster maximum autonomy in students. Paul Robin ran a libertarian orphanage at Cempuis, France, in the late nineteenth century. His school influenced Sébastien Faure, who founded a libertarian school called La Ruche, also in France. In Spain, Francisco Ferrer established Escuela Moderna in 1901. In Germany there were libertarian schools in Hamburg. And in England, the famous Summerhill school is still operating, almost a hundred years after it was started by A.S. Neill.

FRANCIS: Anarchists have established progressive schools in many places. Since the nineteenth century they have been advocating a radical reorganization of schools and education, including co-ed classes and the development of the whole person, integrating manual, technical, intellectual, and artistic skills in the curriculum. It's not too far-fetched to say that anarchists believe the revolution will be born in school as much as in the factory or on the street.

Adult education is equally important. In times and places where most adults were still illiterate, anarchists opened "people's universities," in Argentina, Cuba, Peru, and Egypt. They have also set up reading circles where newspapers and books are read aloud to those who can't read.

Since the nineteenth century, anarchists have also been pushing for a reduction in the power of teachers, by abolishing corporal punishment, limiting discipline, and offering choices to students. A century later these ideas are the norm, though most people don't realize it was anarchists who first developed and tested them. James Guillaume, an anarchist close to Bakunin, argued that students should be allowed to choose their teacher, who "will no longer be a detested tyrant but a friend to whom they will listen with pleasure." Fernand Pelloutier, a revolutionary French trade unionist from the early twentieth century, thought it was essential to open children's eyes to the injustices of liberal society, to train the children of the poor and the exploited in "the science of their misery," and to "teach them to revolt."

Why not encourage autonomy among school children? Guillaume looked forward to the day when "children will be entirely free. They will organize their own games, their talks, systematize their own work, arbitrate disputes, etc." In 2002, during the No Borders campaign, a temporary, autonomous, self-governing camp was established in Strasbourg. Part of the camp was set aside for children. The children sent their own delegates to the general assembly, where they complained that the adults weren't keeping the camp clean and that some adults had pitched their tents in the space set aside for children. When rumours began circulating that the police were preparing to evict the campers, the children declared that they wanted to stay, arguing that it was their camp, too. Their parents intervened and took them away.

The State

THOMAS: Let's talk about the state. Errico Malatesta, an Italian anarchist, says there's a widely held assumption that "government [is] a necessary organ of social life, and that consequently a society without government would be at the mercy of disorder, and fluctuate between the unbridled arrogance of some and the blind vengeance of others." He adds, "since it was thought that government was necessary and that without government there could only be disorder and confusion, it was natural and logical that anarchy, which means absence of government, should sound like absence of order." Malatesta went on to say:

> Anarchists . . . have used the word State . . . to mean the sum total of the political, legislative, judiciary, military, and financial institutions through which the management of their own affairs, the control over their personal behaviour, the responsibility for their personal safety, are taken away from the people and entrusted to others

who, by usurpation or delegation, are vested with the
powers to make the laws for everything and everybody,
and to oblige the people to observe them, if need be, by
the use of collective force.

FRANCIS: Criticism of the state is a distinguishing mark
of anarchism. No other ideology proposes such a radical
critique of the state, with the exception of the ideology of
some orthodox religions that reject any authority other
than God, and the ideology of First Nations traditional-
ists such as Mohawk activist Taiaiake Alfred. He uses the
term "indigenous anarchism" to talk about a movement
among aboriginal peoples to reject the European model
of the state and replace it with autonomous direct action
as the means of political expression.

Recent discussions of the "matrix of domination" and
intersectionality have identified three principle systems of
domination—class, sex, and race. But we could add others, such as sexual identity and orientation, physical ability
and disability, age, etc. The state in itself is never considered a system of domination; it's seen as an institution
that reinforces the various systems, and which sometimes
mitigates the negative effects of a system, for example by
implementing anti-discrimination policies.

Now, the latter point is sometimes used to justify the
state. The argument is that the state is there to protect us
and assure our well-being and happiness. But anarchists
aren't duped. As long as there has been a state, there has
never been equality or freedom: one group governs and
the rest are governed. Our various electoral systems tell us

we're free because we don't have to worry about politics, other people will take care of it for us. In other words, we don't have to worry about making decisions that affect our common affairs. We're supposed to believe we're free when we let other people decide for us. That's absurd. As Kropotkin said, "The best way of being free is not to be represented, not to abandon affairs—all affairs—to Providence or to the elected ones, but to handle them ourselves."

We're told that we need a collective political entity called a country, and that this thing called a country is formed and represented by the state. We're told that the country thinks and acts through the state and its representatives. We're supposed to believe that the state incarnates the country, that the state is what allows the country to exist and the people to make common cause. In fact, the opposite is true. When a state claims to take care of everything, why should I and my fellow citizens get involved in politics? With complete peace of mind, I can retreat into my private life and cultivate my individualism. The state encourages individualism. It encourages each individual to express his or her needs and ask for services. The state treats us as individuals, identifying each of us by a number.

The state is a system of domination over a population and a territory. (Politicians prefer to talk about "sovereignty.") It's a system of oppression by the police, the courts, the prisons, and the army. (Politicians talk about "security" and the need to "maintain law and order.") It's a system of exploitation through taxes, which support a multitude of public servants—me included, because

I teach at a public university. (The politicians ask us to make our "contribution" in order to "distribute wealth" according to the principles of "social justice.") The state is also a system of exclusion. It keeps members of the governed class—you and I—out of the places where power is wielded and decisions are made. (We're only allowed to enter Parliament as visitors.) And it keeps "foreigners" outside our borders. (We can't invite everyone in, we're told.)

For all these reasons, anarchists are opposed to the state and want it abolished. There are two basic approaches to this goal. We can attack the state head-on, through revolution. Or we can free ourselves from its influence and organize on the margins of the state. Gustav Landauer, a German anarchist of Jewish origin, said around 1900: "The state is a social relationship; a certain way of people relating to one another. It can be destroyed by creating new social relationships; i.e., by people relating to one another differently."

It should be clear by now that anarchists have no sympathy for a state controlled by elected politicians. Elections are seen as an aberration, because to vote is essentially to voluntarily choose people to rule over us. The governments we elect pretend to govern in our name and for our benefit, but in fact they impose their will on us by force of law.

In the real world, however, election fever is hard to resist. The media and everyone around us tells us it's "a historic moment," and the coming election is crucial. Some anarchists will vote for a candidate on the left or against a candidate on the right, hoping for the lesser of two evils.

This happened in France in 2002, during the second round of the presidential elections. Anarchists were so horrified at the thought of the extreme-right National Front winning, and Jean-Marie Le Pen becoming president, that they heeded the call to defend the republic and helped elect the candidate of the right, Jacques Chirac. This sparked heated discussion in anarchist circles. (During the second round of the presidential elections in 2017, some French anarchists voted strategically once again, this time for Emmanuel Macron and against Marine Le Pen, the new leader of the National Front.)

Another example, even stranger: anarchists served as cabinet ministers in the Republican government in Spain during the civil war of 1936–39. One of them was Federica Montseny, who we talked about earlier in connection with the Castro regime in Cuba. Montseny was the first woman in Spain to hold a ministerial post, that of health minister. She helped set up orphanages for children and shelters for prostitutes who wanted out of the sex trade. Three other cabinet ministers in the Republican government were anarcho-syndicalists. They even fought at the front against Franco's army. But the decision of these anarchists to become government ministers provoked heated criticism from their comrades.

Personally, I don't vote in elections, though I have in the past. I find the electoral circus too depressing. But it shouldn't be hard for us to agree on this point. You yourself are a bit of an anarchist! You've always been very critical of politicians in general and elections in particular. Didn't you vote for the Rhinoceros Party at some point? If you have such a low opinion of elections, surely you can understand why anarchists tend not to vote and instead urge others to abstain.

THOMAS: You're right, I am a bit of an anarchist—more than a bit, sometimes. What bothers me most about politicians is that they don't respect their own party platform, never mind keep their promises. When I do vote, I vote for a platform. Voting Rhinoceros was voting for a platform that ridiculed the electoral system. Leaving your ballot blank is another kind of protest, a way of saying that none of the candidates interest you. But that implies that if there were a satisfactory candidate, you'd vote for him or her; so you're still participating in the election.

The power of the state manifests itself in laws and the civil servants who apply them; shades of Kafka! Louis XIV of France said: "L'État, c'est moi." (I am the State.) That's not something an ordinary citizen in a democratic country can say. Whether you're on the left or right, if the government in power is of the opposite persuasion there's nothing democratic about being governed by them, by allowing laws that you have no say in formulating to be imposed on you. It's another kind of "silent majority." The power of the state is fundamentally based on numbers, the number of votes. As ordinary citizens, you and I surrender our power to people we don't know, and they take the power.

It seems to me that to abstain from voting is anarchist only if we don't become part of the "silent majority." We have to be a vocal minority. (Once again I recommend the novel *Seeing*, by José Saramago. It deals brilliantly with the question of abstaining by casting a blank ballot.) The only time I truly feel I have a say in things is during a referendum, when I can vote for an idea. Referenda are the only form of direct participation.

FRANCIS: Anarchists are more open to the idea of referenda, because instead of electing a representative you're expressing your opinion on a specific issue. In their assemblies anarchists sometimes use ballots to make decisions, though they prefer to try to reach consensus.

Anarchists usually choose not to vote in elections, for two basic reasons. One is to be politically consistent: if you don't want a leader, why vote for one? The second is for propaganda purposes: announcing one's abstention is a political gesture of defiance against the electoral system.

Anarchists abstain out of disgust, because candidates who claim they want to serve the country or the common good are usually self-centred and hungry for power, privilege, and glory. (If not, why go into politics?) Anarchists abstain out of bitterness, because the electoral game has become so corrupted by money and political debate so influenced by the private and public media that no candidate espousing anarchist ideas has a serious chance of being elected anywhere. Anarchists abstain because we're realistic: we know that our single ballot has no chance, or almost no chance, of influencing the outcome of the election. Anarchists abstain out of pessimism, because we know enough history to know that progressive politicians usually end up betraying their progressive promises once they get into power. We've seen it happen time and again with social democratic parties: since the 1980s they've been moving to the centre or the right. They've adopted a right-wing, neoliberal economic agenda—supporting big business while cutting budgets, cutting social services, and imposing austerity on ordinary people.

It's important to understand that when anarchists choose not to vote, it's not because they think politics is unimportant. On the contrary, anarchists think it's irresponsible to limit politics to a single vote, every four or five years, and let politicians lead us around by the nose the rest of the time. For anarchists, "doing" politics means engaging in concrete action with other people, not leaving politics to our "representatives."

THOMAS: I understand much better now why the primary goal of anarchists is to get rid of the king, the state, or the head of state—because the power of the state (legislative, executive, or judicial) ultimately affects all citizens, whether we like it or not. So let's address the big question now, as Malatesta did: is it possible and desirable to do away completely with governments, and is that likely to happen in the foreseeable future?

Élisée Reclus put it this way:

> It is in fact our struggle against all official power that distinguishes [anarchists] most essentially. Each individuality seems to us to be the centre of the universe and each has the same right to its integral development, without interference from any power that supervises, reprimands or castigates it. . . . Is this truly a noble ideal? Does it justify the sacrifice of dedicated men and all the terrible risks that revolutions inevitably bring in their wake?

So, what do anarchists really mean when they talk about "eliminating the government"? Does that mean we should physically attack the head of state? Or resist the police and the judiciary, who are given authority by the state to apply the laws? Or should we attack the army, which has so much power invested in it by the state that it sometimes feels entitled to stage a coup d'état and overthrow the government? That's happened so many times throughout history that I'm almost ready to believe that it's the police and the army who are the real troublemakers, not the anarchists.

FRANCIS: So you're asking me, is revolution possible? We could ask the same question about the struggle against any system of domination: Is it really possible to overthrow it? Is it desirable? Isn't the risk too great? Too many anarchists have died trying to overthrow the state, because the state, while claiming to rule for our benefit, has proven itself ruthless if we stop obeying it.

Putting aside the revolutionary myths and the dreams of insurrectionists, we know very little about how to actually start a revolution. Why does a revolution start today, and not yesterday or tomorrow? Like many other political groups, anarchists have often been caught unprepared when revolts and revolutions started. For example, anarchist groups lagged far behind other groups in organizing big protest marches in May 1968, and again in 2012 during the *Printemps érable* (maple spring*) student protests in Quebec. Anarchists nevertheless participated in both protests, hoping they might lead to full-scale revolutions.

---

* "Maple spring" is both a reference to *sirop d'érable*, Quebec's traditional spring harvest of maple syrup, and a play on *Printemps arabe*, the "Arab Spring." —Trans.

The relationship between the army and the modern state is very interesting, and tells us a lot about the true nature of the state. Pierre Clastres, an anthropologist, studied how war is conducted in stateless societies. He points to the example of Geronimo, the legendary Apache leader. The Apache didn't consider Geronimo a chief; he was their leader only for military campaigns, and even then he didn't have the power to impose his decisions on his warriors. Once, after a victory over American soldiers, Geronimo tried to persuade his fighters to go on the war path again. Without the means to compel them he could rely only on the persuasive power of his words, which failed: only two warriors agreed to follow him. What a difference from today's modern state, where the politicians who declare war never do the fighting, and soldiers who refuse to fight are severely punished, or even shot.

THOMAS: Indeed, soldiers who refuse to fight are considered traitors to their country, while the politicians who declare war and put their country at risk are honoured.

FRANCIS: The state as we know it today was born out of war, at the end of the Middle Ages. Political authority thus equates with military authority: the king and the feudal lords were, above all, warriors who provided military protection to the population in exchange for taxes and free labour. The fortified castle was the site of political power. As the centuries passed, wars became more and more expensive as weapons became increasingly sophisticated (guns, battleships, etc.). Kingdoms created bureaucracies to better organize their resources, be they financial resources (statistics on jobs, revenues, etc.), human resources (registers of births and deaths, demographic statistics), or material resources (control over natural resources, development of transportation infrastructure such as ports, bridges, roads). Thus the modern state was born. Local citizens' assemblies and professional guilds were abandoned or even outlawed by the state. The king appointed officials to administer municipalities. As time went on, politics became separate from military power, which finally became submissive to the civil power of the state.

The twentieth century was both a century of totalitarianism (Stalinism, Naziism, Maoism) and a century of liberalism. In both cases, the state as a political entity triumphed; it now overlays the whole planet and impacts the lives of almost everyone. But the twentieth century also saw mass slaughters by the state: the First and Second World Wars, the wars of decolonization, the Iran–Iraq war, the war in the Congo, to name just a few. The result: millions of deaths in wars waged by states, not to mention the genocides, the dropping of atomic bombs on civilians by a liberal state, and all the civil wars involving the armed forces of various states. In fact, in some countries in Latin America, the armed forces of the state have spent more time massacring their own citizens than fighting foreign armies.

THOMAS: What's more, politicians commit their countries to waging war or invading other countries without consulting their citizens or their armies, or seeking authorization from government bodies. And now, under the guise of "national security," a nebulous term, governments can surveil or detain citizens for the slightest suspicion. The government of the United States even uses drones to execute people it considers enemies, without charge or trial—and in the process kills countless innocent civilians.

FRANCIS: Good point. The scale of violence in the twentieth century exceeded anything in human history, with over two hundred million deaths from inter-state conflicts— and the twenty-first century isn't looking much better. States are becoming more and more powerful, intrusive, and violent. And still we tell ourselves that we need states to stop us from massacring one another.

Whether states are controlled by civilians or the military, they always have "the monopoly of the legitimate use of physical force," as the sociologist Max Weber put it. And it remains a system of domination, oppression, exploitation, and exclusion. Sometimes the army tries to take the place of the civilian elite, especially when a country is threatened by leftist forces or torn apart by ethnic rivalries, or sometimes leftist forces take over the state in an armed revolution. That's what happened with the Bolsheviks in Russia, Mao in China, Castro in Cuba: the state remained, but the bureaucracy, the army, the police, the judges, and the prison guards all became communist. Even though there was a revolution, the state continued to be a system of domination, oppression, exploitation, and exclusion. The Red Army in the Soviet Union didn't hesitate to massacre its anarchist comrades.

Anarchists are generally anti-militarist. They have often taken up the cause of people opposing compulsory military service, at the risk of ending up behind bars themselves. Emma Goldman was thrown into prison for distributing anti-war propaganda in the United States during the First World War. In France in 1984, when military service was still obligatory, a draft dodger named Patrick Aguiar said at his trial:

> I refuse to support any army; they are forces of destruction. I refuse military service; it prepares people for war; it teaches people to kill and to blindly obey. I am for the abolition of armies and weapons. . . . My life belongs to me, and I insist on freedom of thought and the freedom to act according to my principles. I am for an anarchist society, that is, a society opposed to all forms of power and based on peace and freedom.

The anarchist network in France actively supported draft dodgers, both those who went to prison and those who went underground. The networks they established to help draft dodgers included doctors who would treat fugitives without informing on them.

But what about you? You weren't an anarchist, but you refused to do your military service during the Algerian War. What made you become a draft dodger?

THOMAS: Well, first let me say that I agree with Patrick Aguiar. At the time of the Algerian War, military service in France lasted twenty-seven months. When I received my call-up I was in Canada, doing an engineering internship. Without consciously thinking about it, I had already made up my mind not to learn to shoot my fellow human beings. I'd come to that conclusion long before. I didn't have the instinct of a warrior, and I had no interest in learning how to march. So when my draft letter arrived, I decided to ignore it. I became a draft dodger. Was I a conscientious objector, too? The line between the two is very thin. In any case, it's a decision I've never regretted. Essentially, I chose not to obey the authority of the state, which was ordering me to serve in its army. Instead, I obeyed a principle I still hold to: "Thou shalt not kill." So, did I just replace one authority with another authority?

FRANCIS: The fundamental question for anarchists is not whether to obey principles. Most anarchists I know are already people of principle, sometimes inflexibly so. The question is who decides the principles. If you want to feel free and autonomous in your moral choices you have to be able to decide for yourself what your principles are, and change them if you want. If an authority insists that you obey certain principles, and punishes you if you don't, then you're not free, even if the principles themselves are worthwhile. Of course, it's very difficult to know whether a particular principle that I uphold is one that I discovered for myself, or whether it was instilled in me through socialization and education, i.e., from my parents, my teachers, and the culture in general.

In your case, it sounds like you followed your conscience and more or less decided on your own that the army wasn't for you and you didn't want to kill people you'd never met who'd done you no harm.

THOMAS: So, does that make me an anarchist? Incidentally, and ironically, even though in theory punishments for military crimes never expire, a few years later the French state granted an amnesty to draft dodgers like me.

FRANCIS: Don't get confused here! Just because one element in a situation sounds anarchist, it doesn't mean the whole situation is anarchist. It's not enough to be against the army to be an anarchist. You know the problem of arguing by syllogism. For example: (1) All cats have moustaches. (2) Hitler had a moustache. (3) Therefore, Hitler was a cat. In the same way, one could argue: (1) Anarchists are against the army. (2) I'm against the army. (3) Therefore, I'm an anarchist. But anarchism isn't that simple. There are other factors to consider before calling someone an anarchist. For example, anarchists are for cooperation and self-management. But even there, you have to be careful. The shareholders of a large insurance, pharmaceutical, or oil company can't claim to be anarchists just because they make decisions about the management of the company in a general assembly.

In another syllogistic fallacy, some people accuse anarchists of playing into the hands of liberalism and even neo-liberalism, especially after May '68 and the emergence of the counter-culture. Why? Because neo-liberalism *also* encourages networking and preaches individual freedom unobstructed by institutions such as the family. There's even a label now, "liberal-libertarian," to designate anarchists who sound just like neo-liberals. But this conflating of *libertarian* and *neoliberal* is false, for two reasons.

First, neo-liberals think engaging in politics is a waste of time for the vast majority of the population. They think the world is a better place when the majority let a clique of experts run the show, and the rest of us are left to enjoy our freedom, at work and in our private life. As long ago as the early nineteenth century, Benjamin Constant, a French liberal, tried to draw a distinction between freedom in the modern sense and freedom as it was understood in previous ages. The ancient Greeks considered themselves free if and only if they could participate in assemblies in the agora and make political decisions collectively. With the advent of modernity and liberalism this idea of freedom was abandoned, according to Constant, and individuals began to consider themselves free if they were *not* obliged to get involved in politics, knowing that a representative or a head of state would do it for them.

This latter idea of freedom is very appealing, especially to "modern" people who complain that activist meetings and assemblies are boring and take too much time. But Constant's analysis contains at least three weaknesses: first, he neglects to mention that capitalism demands we work long hours, leaving little time for politics; second, entrusting power to people who might then manage public affairs for their private benefit is problematic, to say the least; and lastly, contrary to Constant's claim, many "modern" people do practice politics through direct engagement and feel liberated when they meet and act collectively. Western modernity is teeming with examples of social movements run by general assemblies, and citizens' groups forming popular assemblies in times of crisis. For example: trade unions; the feminist movement; the soviets and workers' assemblies in Germany and Hungary around 1920; popular assemblies in Budapest in 1956 and Prague in 1968, the large assemblies held by protest movements in May '68, and more recently, the international Occupy movement and the anti-austerity Indignados movement in Spain.

There's a second reason why it's wrong to conflate *libertarian* and *neoliberal*. Neoliberalism advocates individual freedom with no other objective than to *have*—in other words, to accumulate and consume goods and wealth—whereas the individual freedom of anarchism must go hand in hand with equality and mutual aid. For anarchists, to *be* and to *act* collectively are more important than to *have* individually. Anarchists consider it essential to get involved in politics collectively. Their networks are aimed precisely at maximizing their political effectiveness, not at maximizing their capital or their consumption. It's important not to mistake neoliberal for libertarian—they're very different, even though they share one or two similarities.

Let's return to the question of war and the military. Many anarchists have been pacifists and advocated non-violence, while others have participated in armed struggles. But even anarchist militias try to uphold the principles of freedom and equality, as they did during the Spanish Civil War.

THOMAS: Yes, the Spanish Civil War is a beautiful example of anarchism put into practice. As Préposiet wrote in his *Histoire de l'anarchisme* (History of anarchism): "The masses remained faithful to the anti-authoritarian ideal . . . an ideal introduced into Spain in the nineteenth century by Bakunin and his followers."

But things are never that simple, are they? The Spanish

Civil War was very complicated. There was a civil war within the civil war, following the rapid rise of the Spanish Communist Party and its alliance with the Republicans. There were the independence movements in the Basque country and in Catalonia. The war inspired writers such as Ernest Hemingway, who wrote *For Whom The Bell Tolls*, and artists such as Pablo Picasso, whose painting *Guernica*, incited by the horrific German bombing of the Basque town of that name, became a symbol of the tragedy of the entire civil war. And let's not forget Montjuïc Castle in Barcelona, where both sides in the war tortured and executed their prisoners. An army of anarchists may be "beautiful" in theory, but it was still an army fighting another army of fellow citizens.

FRANCIS: Yes, that's true. But the anarchists tried, whenever possible, to stick to their principles. Their militias either had no officers or the officers were elected by the troops and could be dismissed by them. German anarchists who fought for the Republic banned saluting in their units and insisted everyone be paid the same. The Italian anarchists refused any pay at all, saying they didn't want to get in the habit of earning a living from war. Anarchist women took part in the fighting at the beginning, though later they were excluded from combat units. Freedom of speech and freedom of the press were allowed, even at the front.

Some people are quick to dismiss all that, saying, "That's all well and good, but the anarchists were massacred in the end." Yes, they were. But it's hard to know if that was due to the way they were organized or external factors. The anarchists received almost no support from their allies within the Republic, and often faced superior enemy forces. They were sent to the most dangerous fronts but received almost no heavy weapons, which were reserved for Republican militias that pledged allegiance to the Soviet Union. The Republican government seized every opportunity to suppress the anarchists. And internationally, the liberal "democracies," including France and Britain, refused to get involved even though Franco's Nationalists were receiving military support from Nazi Germany and fascist Italy.

THOMAS: Let's talk about the police, now. The state delegates authority to the police, who in turn enforce laws and regulations. What do anarchists say about that?

FRANCIS: What do you think they say?

THOMAS: That the police are the most visible organ of the state, the one most present in our daily lives. That they're the symbol of authority that represses us more than any other, and so when they overstep their authority, anarchists are quick to attack it.

FRANCIS: Exactly. Anarchists are especially critical because historically the police have always harassed and attacked them. Bakunin, Louise Michel, Kropotkin, and Goldman all spent time in prison and, in some cases, were forced into exile. Italian anarchists were among the first to be imprisoned by Mussolini, but when the dictator fell the new government didn't set them free; instead the anarchists were interned in camps, to neutralize them. Anarchists in the alter-globalization movement today are frequently singled out for police repression. Thousands of anarchists have been arrested, either alone or in large groups during demonstrations.

So police repression is one problem. But anarchists also consider the police a professional organization that, like the armed forces, is incompatible with anarchist ideals of freedom, equality, solidarity, and mutual aid. Both the police and the army are authoritarian, hierarchical organizations; on principle, they deny their members' autonomy. They demand blind obedience: their members must be prepared to kill or be killed by complete strangers. You're even rewarded with medals and promotions when you kill. And yet we're told that it's the anarchists who are violent, and it's the state that guarantees peace and security!

Police forces as we know them are a fairly recent creation. They first appeared in France and Great Britain around the nineteenth century, chiefly to protect the rich from the poor. The Scottish philosopher Adam Smith, one of the key thinkers in modern, liberal economics, said: "Civil government, so far as it is instituted for the security of property, is in reality instituted for the defence of the rich against the poor." He also said, "It is only under the shelter of the civil magistrate that the owner of . . . valuable property . . . can sleep a single night in security." Anarchists are in complete agreement with liberals here. As Malatesta said, "Without the gendarme the property owner could not exist."

Anarchists are often asked how society could function

without the police. Here's what anarchists say: if you want to maintain the gap between the rich and the poor, between those who dominate and those who are dominated, then yes, you need a police force (either public or private) to protect the rich and put the poor in prison where they can do no harm. But there would be much less need for police in an anarchist society, because there would no longer be a state, or private property, or dominants and dominated, or rich and poor. There would be much less crime to prevent, and less need for punishment. Who would disobey whom? Whom would there be to steal from?

Anarchists reject the dominant ideology, which sees a person first as a potential murderer, rapist, or thief. This fear surfaces repeatedly in the political philosophy inspired by Thomas Hobbes and social Darwinism. It finds expression in the mass media, in crime shows, horror movies, and thrillers. Anarchists believe there would be much less violence in society if there were justice, freedom, and equality.

People inevitably ask: what would an anarchist society do if a maniac with a chainsaw attacked someone? Well, in that case, the community would come together and find a solution. The culprit might be forced into exile, or required to go to therapy. Or there might be a collective ritual of reconciliation and rehabilitation. A volunteer emergency response team might be set up to intervene in future calls for help. If you don't like those ideas, or have alternatives to suggest, as a member of the community you'd be welcome to speak in the assembly and participate in the decision-making. The goal is to manage these kinds of crises collectively, rather than letting the police and the judges take over and impose law and order on the community.

But then critics say, "community justice is dangerous, it can turn into a lynch mob!" Well, what about police interventions, which are often brutal and racist? What about all the judges who are in bed with the dominant class (which they belong to)? Anarchists aren't fools. They know the current justice system—the police, the courts, and the prisons—is a human disaster. Prisons have become "schools of crime," as the saying goes. Let's face it: throwing a nasty person in a room and locking the door is a complete failure of imagination on the part of society.

THOMAS: We could talk about the army and the police all night. We could talk about extreme forms of the police, such as the Gestapo, or in Russia the Cheka and the GPU, who executed anarchists and other enemies of the revolution. But I think you've said enough for me to make up my own mind now, and I'd like to move on to other questions.

We've barely touched on another kind of authority, another manifestation of state power, and that is the civil service. For most of us, dealing with civil servants and accessing the public services they administer is our only direct contact with the state, apart from once every few years when we can vote. But when I think of the civil service, what immediately come to mind are Kafka and Big Brother. Kafka's novel *The Trial* depicts the justice system as a terrifying, opaque world, weighted down by hierarchy and bureaucracy. Another of his novels, *The Castle*, shows the futility of trying to penetrate an infinitely complex bureaucracy. The idea of Big Brother comes from George Orwell's novel *Nineteen Eighy-Four*, which depicts an all-powerful state that controls everything and everyone. In some ways, that seems to be already happening.

FRANCIS: Anarchists today, especially in the West, are in a paradoxical position vis-à-vis the state. They waver between two notions that are not mutually exclusive. The first and most widely held is that the state exists to protect the bourgeoisie and capitalism—and to that end maintains an army, the police, judges, and prisons—while also providing social services like health care, education, and unemployment insurance to help win over and subjugate the middle classes and the disadvantaged.

This has certainly been the case since the rise of the welfare state in the late nineteenth century, which can partially be explained by the fear of revolution; the first social welfare policies were implemented by Bismarck in Germany to defuse a possible worker's revolt. The welfare state expanded dramatically after the Second World War, during which an economist named Sir William Beveridge presented a report to the British parliament that said, "Each individual citizen is more likely to concentrate upon his war effort if he feels that his Government will be ready in time with plans for that Better world." And so the welfare state was built to reward the British people for their sacrifices during the war. The liberal elites also feared that people would be drawn to the social model offered by the Soviet Union, which came out of the war glorified by its heroic resistance to the Nazi armies (remember the epic battle of Stalingrad). As well, communists had actively fought in the underground resistance against the Nazis across Europe, and remained influential after the war.

Since the 1980s, anarchists have joined with other progressive forces to defend social welfare programs and resist the spending cuts and austerity imposed by conservative, neo-liberal, and even social democratic parties. Anarchists have always tried to improve the living conditions of the working class and the middle class.

The second notion of the state put forward by anarchists today is much more critical, even taking social-democratic states to task. Anarchists holding this view (and sometimes they're the same anarchists who support the first notion) see social services and the bureaucracy as part of the machinery of power that serves to normalize, control, and discipline the population, weakening its will to revolt. Social services and the bureaucracy encourage individualism: rather than act collectively to help each other, individuals deal directly with the state, on their own. The most critical anarchists remind us that even social-democratic states always serve the interests of capitalism by providing enormous benefits to private companies, defending their interests through international trade agreements, tax exemptions, and direct and indirect subsidies (for example, by providing transportation and communication networks, and training a skilled workforce).

The state consists of a governing class, which dominates, oppresses, and exploits the governed class. Obviously there are significant differences in the power wielded by the president or prime minister of a country, a judge, a police officer, a civil servant working for the Ministry of the Environment, a postman, and a teacher in a public school. But each in his or her way belongs to the governing class and lives off the exploitation of the rest of the population, even if they provide services in return. In a similar way, capitalism also claims to provide services to society, such as a salary for the exploited work, and goods and services in exchange for a price. Maia Ramnath, an anarchist from India who lives in the United States, says the state is "a mechanism designed to accumulate wealth in order to make war, to make war in order to protect its wealth, and to make laws to facilitate its functioning, meaning to protect its own stability. This includes the maintenance of a reasonable degree of contentment among its members." Seen from this perspective, the state is more than just an institution that protects the rich and defends private property.

THOMAS: So the state cannot be seen to be protecting only the bourgeoisie and capitalism. It must act as if it's protecting the working class, too, by being some form of welfare state.

FRANCIS: Yes, it's the old carrot and stick approach. Speaking of the welfare state, the most contentious issue for anarchists today is the question of taxes and income tax. We hear a lot of rabble-rousing from the neoliberal right about reducing taxes. On the other side of the fence, there's a consensus among many progressive forces that income taxes are desirable because they help redistribute wealth from the rich to the poor. But more than a hundred years ago Kropotkin argued that by imposing taxes the state was in effect forcing every citizen to work for the state. He wrote: "The amount of work given every year by the producer to the state must be enormous. It must reach, and for certain classes exceed, the three days work a week that the serf used to give his lord." For Kropotkin, work in the form of taxes was another kind of exploitation.

Progressive people are alarmed by this kind of thinking. "What are you proposing?" they ask. "Do you want services like health care and education to be provided by private companies?" There, in a nutshell, is the essential tragedy of the twentieth and early twenty-first centuries—we in the West are incapable of thinking outside the dichotomy of public-versus-private. We believe that services can only be provided by either the state or by capitalism. It's sad how blind we are, because there are other economic systems capable of producing goods and services.

The patriarchy wants women to produce goods and services within the family for free. It wants women to take care of the children, the sick, and the elderly, feed them and clean the home, and all for free—even if it's unjust and sometimes illegal. And yet they oppose paying for this kind of work in the public system or in the private marketplace.

THOMAS: There's also volunteering, a form of unpaid work that's framed in terms of "being helpful." Volunteers

put themselves at the service of society and the state out
of a sense of solidarity. But they sometimes do tasks that
should be provided by the state, or at least by paid workers. It would be interesting to know which economies are
dragged down by volunteers.

FRANCIS: In fact, anarchists strongly encourage working
for free. But volunteering is a special kind of unpaid work.
As you point out, volunteers cover up the failures of capitalism and the state. And let's not forget that it's women
who do most of the unpaid work in society, which seems
to indicate that they're driven to it by the social structure
and the patriarchy.

As for the dichotomy between public and private,
ever since the nineteenth century anarchists have been
proposing a third option, "the commons." Marianne
Enckell, who helps manage a library in Lausanne, Switzerland, called Centre international de recherches sur
l'anarchisme (International centre for research on anarchism), points out that the anarchists who participated in
the 1874 congress of the Federalist International Work-
ingmen's Association, in Brussels, proposed that "public
services" be provided not by an "omnipotent State" but
by autonomous, federated communes, functioning on the
principle of mutual aid. The tragedy of the West today
is that there are almost no more communally held economic resources; there is no commons. Everything has
been either privatized or nationalized, which in the latter
case means monopolized by the state under the name of
"public property."

The Origins of Human Communities

THOMAS: I'd like to talk about what kind of government anarchists envision. I've been reading a book by the French historian Roland Mousnier called *Monarchies et royautés: De la préhistoire à nos jours* (Monarchies and royalties: from prehistory to our times). If I'm understanding him correctly, the first form of leadership or authority in human societies around the world was the head of the tribe or clan. Then came the monarchs and various royalties, such as the Egyptian pharaohs, the kings and queens of Europe, and the emperors of China and Japan. This form of authority lasted for thousands of years in the case of the pharaohs and emperors, hundreds of years for the European monarchs. The right to reign was always claimed to emanate from the spirits or the gods. The pharaoh was considered a divine priest, the European kings and queens claimed divine authority, the Chinese emperors were called the "Son of Heaven," and the Japanese emperor is still called the "Heavenly Sovereign." There are still "divine" royalties reigning in thirty-odd countries around the world, though most are in Asia and Europe. That brings me to this question: Is it possible to have anarchy in a society where the chief, the king, the monarch, the sovereign, or the emperor claims to be acting in the name of a god? In other words, in order for anarchy to exist, does there have to be a separation of church and state? As Bakunin said: "Slaves of God, men must also be slaves of Church and State, *in so far as the State is consecrated by the Church.*"

FRANCIS: No one knows how communities from the dawn of humanity were organized politically. Anarchists like Kropotkin encourage us to remember the positive role of mutual aid throughout human history. But a general theory of history doesn't flow from that. Personally, I'm wary of histories that claim humanity evolved in stages, from the family to the clan to the tribe to royalty to empire, etc. That said, many anarchists believe (as do Marxists and liberals) that the state is secondary, that it arose after the appearance of private property, in order to protect private property. Adam Smith said that in a country with rich people and poor people, there has to be a state so the police can guarantee the rich a good night's sleep, without fear of being robbed by the poor. What Smith regarded as a practical solution, anarchists consider an unjust collusion between the rich and the state.

Some anthropologists and historians date the birth of the state to the beginning of agriculture and the possibility of surplus production. For our purposes, that's not very helpful because it's a universalizing theory that sees human history as homogeneous, when I think it's much more complex. To be honest, I'm not an expert on human history and I can't say whether the Chinese state, which is very old, or the Egyptian state, or the Ethiopian, or the pre-Columbian states, or the Aztecs all had the same origin and the same history. And then, what about city states, like Athens in Ancient Greece; or Florence, Venice and Pisa during the Renaissance? And what about empires—are they states?

Anarchists like Kropotkin and Landauer remind us that modern European states such as England and France did not exist in the Middle Ages. There were only kings ruling over their realms, with the help of a few bureaucrats and soldiers. The king didn't actually do much, other than throw parties, marry off his children, appoint people to various positions, award monopolies, wage war, and exploit his kingdom. He didn't provide what we call public services, such as health care, education, culture, industry, or environmental protection. The state as such didn't develop in Europe until the end of the Middle Ages, when kings needed more resources to wage war. To that end, they built up large civil administrations. It was these nascent states that would later colonize North America, where according to anarchist anthropologists, the Indigenous people were living in a free and egalitarian manner—in other words, in a way that resembled anarchy.

THOMAS: That's very interesting because when we take a narrow view of history, we lose sight of the whole. That's certainly true of the so-called "discovery" of the Americas, which is usually told from the point of view of Columbus and almost never from the perspective of the people he "discovered." There are exceptions, of course. Howard Zinn starts his book *A People's History of the United States* with a chapter entitled "Columbus, the Indians, and Human Progress," in which he claims that the Europeans committed genocide in the Americas. In the same spirit, Amin Maalouf wrote *The Crusades Through Arab Eyes*.

FRANCIS: The way we are socialized encourages us to take the point of view of the leaders and the dominants:

we learn the history of the kings, queens, and conquerors; we watch movies and TV shows about the police and the military. In the media, politicians and business leaders do most of the talking. We believe the media when they say "The United States has decided . . . " or "France has declared . . . " even though, in fact, it's only the president of the United States or France, or a government minister, who is speaking,

Religions

THOMAS: But what about my question about the relationship between church and state?

FRANCIS: Ah, yes, I forgot . . . Religious communities often included people who claimed to be able to interpret the signs of the gods, and even speak to the community on behalf of the gods. But communities risked being dominated, either spiritually or materially, by a person claiming these special powers. Some communities counterbalanced their religious leader and their military leader, to neutralize any ambitions that one or the other might have. Sometimes, the women put themselves forward as guardians of the community's spiritual values. Giving women that role helped, at least in part, to offset their inequality in economic and political matters.

Some Christians are sympathetic to anarchism, such as Leo Tolstoy and the French philosopher Jacques Ellul. They call themselves Christian anarchists, and see anarchism as inherent in Christianity. They point out that Jesus was a preacher who criticized the rich and the elites, promoted equality and non-violence, and sided with the poor and the prostitutes.

You're right that empires and kingdoms sustained themselves for centuries and sometimes millennia by claiming divine authority, which ensured their legitimacy and enhanced their prestige. During the nineteenth century, European anarchists denounced both the Christian church and the state, whether monarchist or republican, and the linkages between them. During the Spanish Revolution of 1936–39, the Catholic church sided with landowners and their hired thugs against the impoverished and exploited peasants. Anarchists responded by shooting priests and burning churches. But note that the anarchists burned the churches; they didn't loot them. They refused to appropriate assets that the church had accumulated through the exploitation of a poor and gullible population.

I mentioned Jewish anarchists earlier. They lived under the authority of Christian states. They expressed their atheism and their anticlericalism by deliberately provoking rabbis and members of the Jewish community, for example by eating pork outside a synagogue.

Why are so many anarchists staunch atheists? There are two reasons, the first political: because the church and religious authorities are in bed with the state. The church gives the state a moral legitimacy. The church also defuses the justifiable anger of the people, diverting it from rebellion to spiritual aspiration by telling people that their poverty and suffering assure them a place in heaven.

The other reason is economic; the church exploits people. Places of worship are built with free labour, and money collected from the faithful funds the lavish lifestyles of the religious elite.

THOMAS: I'd like to look more closely at anarchy and religion. So many questions come to mind. Is the situation the same for the three most common religions in the West—Christianity, Judaism, and Islam? Can a believer, someone totally devoted to his god and his dogma, be an anarchist? Or is someone who criticizes any aspect of her religion therefore a skeptic or a heretic? A key question for me is who, ultimately, is responsible for the social status of men and women: religions or the silent majority of non-believers? Can a true believer be an anarchist? Surely not, if being an anarchist means advocating the abolition of the authority of God and renouncing religion and faith.

I've been reading Jacque Ellul's book, *Anarchism and Christianity*. He claims the Bible supports a convergence between anarchism and Christianity. He says there has always been a "Christian anarchism" and that it's pacifist, anti-nationalist, anti-capitalist, and moral. For Ellul, God is love, anarchy is love, therefore . . .

FRANCIS: There's no question that the teachings of Jesus Christ, as reported in the Bible, embody the principles of anarchism. Some historians also maintain that anarchism was manifest in the millenarian movements of the Middle Ages, when peasants rebelled against the religious hierarchy and corrupt landowners, pooled their land and property, and practiced equality between the sexes. Ellul says that the Catholic church perverted this essentially just and legitimate message, establishing instead a hierarchical institution that brainwashes and exploits people.

THOMAS: In fact, my question is not so much about anarchy and religion, as about anarchy within religion. To put it another way, are certain religions (such as Catholicism, which is very hierarchical) more likely than others to provoke an anarchist awakening? And if someone protests against the authority of the church, is he just being anticlerical, an iconoclast, or a heretic?

FRANCIS: Good questions! I'm not an expert on religions, so I can't give you a detailed answer. But some historians of anarchy say that traces of anarchism can be found in the Taoist philosophy and religion of the ancient Chinese sage, Laozi. I know that the Jewish prophets denounced the corruption of the religious, political, and economic elites of the day, citing the words of God. Some people say that the Christian concept of the New Covenant fundamentally advocates equality, freedom, and solidarity. And certainly the words attributed to Jesus can be used to justify anarchism, or at the very least a critique of hierarchy in all its forms. I think it was André Malraux who said that Jesus was the only successful anarchist.

THOMAS: What I meant was: can a believer be an anarchist if he rejects some other form of authority, such as the state, while remaining a believer and thus submitting to a supreme authority?

FRANCIS: That's a theoretical question. Some anarchists, such as Bakunin, argue that it's theoretically impossible to believe in a god or gods and be an anarchist. That's because the existence of a god is inconsistent with the free will of humans, and thus with our autonomy, a principle dear to all anarchists. Bakunin said: "If God is, man is a slave; now, man can and must be free; then, God does not exist." Seen from that perspective, it's impossible to believe in God and be an anarchist, even if some religious values and anarchist principles overlap.

THOMAS: As an atheist, I agree. I don't see how a true believer, someone who blindly submits to a supreme authority, can free himself from that authority, even partially. Doing so would mean rejecting the dogmas of the religion and therefore repudiating one's faith.

FRANCIS: Bakunin also said that history demonstrates that "priests of all religions, except those of persecuted faiths, have always been the allies of tyranny." But I must stress this point: anarchism is an all-encompassing vision. It cannot be reduced to a few parts, or one or two principles. That's the trap of syllogistic logic that I talked about earlier: cats have moustaches, Hitler had a moustache— comparing the two is pointless.

If slave-owners form an independent association in which all the members are equal and act in solidarity (that is, in solidarity with other slave-owners, not with their slaves), obviously that doesn't make them anarchists, because they continue to dominate their slaves. If someone is a Christian and helps the poor, that's great; but if that person continues to say that we should take the Pope's word as truth and obey it without exercising our free will, then that's not anarchism.

The Catholic church is a hierarchical organization, with distinct levels of authority (pope, cardinals, bishops, etc.). It fosters inequality by ensuring its elites live in luxury, and practices flagrant sexism by barring women from positions of authority. Anyone who operates within the Catholic church, and especially someone who rises up through the hierarchy, cannot—in my view—be an anarchist in the literal sense of the word.

So that's the theory. In fact, I know at least one militant anarchist who works for the Catholic church and believes in God. He's critical of the institution, but he works for it, for a salary, just as many anarchists work for capitalist companies. We all have to pay the rent and buy the groceries. There are very few pure anarchists nowadays. Most of us participate in some way or another in the statist or capitalist system, accepting a salary from an employer and paying our taxes and income taxes.

However, some anarchists participate as little as possible in the system, living in poverty, living in squats, eating food thrown out by supermarkets and restaurants. The militant Catholic anarchist I just mentioned thinks that those who truly put into practice the will of God as he understands it are the anarchists working for freedom, equality, and solidarity against all forms of domination, inequality, and injustice.

THOMAS: What about worker priests? Do they challenge the fundamental structures of society or the dogmas of their religion?

FRANCIS: Yes, at least in part. But very few of the anarchists I know talk about religion or God. It's generally taken for granted that anarchists are atheists and that religion is a problem, not a solution.

The question becomes more complicated when you look at aboriginal resistance struggles in the Americas. These movements practice solidarity, mutual aid, and traditional consensus decision-making, but often take their inspiration from traditional Native spirituality. It's hard for anarchists coming from a Western European tradition to sincerely respect these movements, because the anarchist tradition is more materialist and suspicious of all forms of spiritual belief and practice. For example, anarchists in Quebec organized a speaking tour of the province for two militant aboriginal Guatemalans. The anarchists were very impressed with the man's experiences as a revolutionary syndicalist, but were uncomfortable with the spiritual meaning that the woman gave to her militant experiences. Yet many aboriginal women play an important role in resistance struggles and protests in Latin America, and their militancy often goes hand in hand with an intense spirituality. Erica Lagalisse, a militant anarchist anthropologist, has proposed a new concept, anarcha-indigenism (rather than anarcho-indigenism), in reference to anarcha-feminism, thus emphasizing the important role of these women.

THOMAS: Is there a place for atheists in society today? In Canada, the United States, and France, people have long debated the role of religion in society. They debate how tolerant society should be of different religions, and whether schools should teach one particular religion or comparative religion. In Quebec, for example, there is ongoing controversy over a required course for all elementary and high school students called Ethics and Religious Culture. Catholic parents even went so far as to challenge the course in the courts. In the height of ridiculousness, the teacher's manual for the course attempts to demonstrate impartiality by assigning exactly the same number of lines to each of the three Abrahamic religions, Christianity, Islam, and Judaism.

So how should society treat atheist parents and students when all religions consider atheism sinful, and the Catholic church says atheists go straight to hell? My parents paid for private lessons in Hebrew so I could pass my bar mitzvah at age thirteen. But I was educated in France in the secular, public school system, where religion wasn't taught. Recently I felt I wanted to understand religion better, so for the first time in my life I read the Old Testament, the New Testament, and the Koran. Then I read *Atheist Manifesto: The Case Against Christianity, Judaism, and Islam* by the French philosopher Michel Onfray, and topped it off with *Pour et contre la Bible* (For and against the Bible), by Sylvain Maréchal, the French essayist. Even today, religious authorities monopolize or heavily influence much of the public debate, not just on education but on other issues like abortion, homosexual rights, and the wearing of the Muslim veil. We're always talking about the rights of believers in the public domain; shouldn't we also be talking about the rights of atheists?

FRANCIS: In the nineteenth century, anarchists advocated secular education and attached great importance to the teaching of the sciences. They saw it as a way to free young people from the false beliefs instilled in them by religious authorities. Anarchists today hesitate to glorify science, knowing the problems it created in the twentieth century, especially nuclear energy. But anarchists certainly favour limiting the influence of religion in the public domain. Anarchists argue that faith should remain a personal matter, and that neither the beliefs nor the precepts of a religion should be imposed on others.

That said, anarchists today are very concerned about the rise of Islamophobia in the West and the stigmatization of Muslim women who wear the veil. This comes at a time when the West is still encumbered by its postcolonial heritage and is openly at war with Islamic "terrorism" (inflamed, of course, by Western interventions in Afghanistan, Iraq, and Mali). It's absurd to call a woman's veil a threat to Western civilization.

THOMAS: The three Abrahamic religions are based on the Bible, the Torah, and the Koran, sacred texts that were written by men and in which God, Yahweh, and Allah speak directly and only to men. All three texts say women were created after men and women's roles are defined by their relationship to men. Not surprisingly, all societies that have been influenced by these three religions are patriarchal societies.

In the Catholic church only men are allowed to be priests, and priests claim to be the sole representatives of "our Father who art in heaven." In traditional Jewish synagogues, women worship in a separate section from men, and only men can read from the Torah (though Reform

Judaism accepts women and gay rabbis, and same-sex marriage). In mosques, Muslim women can only pray with the permission of men, and must obey certain rules. Thus, in all three religions, as traditionally practiced, and especially among fundamentalists, authority is held by the men and women are considered second-class. This affects all of society, which has a long way to go to achieve moral, religious, and sexual equality between women and men. Women's struggles, such as for abortion rights, are far from over, and anarchists active on these issues have a long road ahead of them.

FRANCIS: You're absolutely right: religions are misogynist, even if some are more misogynist than others, and even if some marginal denominations such as the Quakers offer more autonomy and equality for women. In Catholicism, women founded orders and monasteries, and during and after the Middle Ages they managed large agricultural properties autonomously, by themselves. But religion is not the sole cause of patriarchy.

THOMAS: Let's go back to the list we made earlier of the different forms of authority—parental authority, state authority, religious authority, the patriarchy, employers and money, and racism. We've covered the first three. Let's look closer at the patriarchy now. Men exercise authority in two ways: first and foremost over women, of course, but also over children through what we might call the authority of fathers. But in their authority over women, I can't think of a single country anywhere in the world that isn't patriarchal.

FRANCIS: Yes, it's true: for all our fine talk about equality of the sexes, Western societies are still patriarchal. Let's face it, even in our family home mother still does almost all of the unpaid domestic work. I don't remember ever cooking or doing the laundry when I was living at home with you two.

THOMAS: You're right, and there's no excuse for it, not even the fact that society in those days was structured to encourage those roles. I grew up in a patriarchal society, but with a strong female presence; my mother was the authority figure in the house when I was young. So I should have behaved differently when I married.

FRANCIS: The belief that some women—a mother or grandmother—are the authority figures at home needs examining more closely. It's important to distinguish between individual personality traits, on the one hand, and the effects of systems of domination, on the other. Even in a patriarchal society, there can be women of strong character who appear to be running the home, ruling over more timid and therefore less authoritarian men. But if you look closer, you see that even those timid men know they are going to be served, that they are going to benefit from the unpaid domestic work of their wives, and that they alone will enjoy the benefits that come with a paid job and a bigger bank account. They will be the owners of the house and car. Even if the husband is unemployed, the wife usually does more of the domestic work and parenting. If a timid man is offered a job that requires the family to move, his wife will follow him, but the opposite is not necessarily true. If the couple start a small business, the timid husband will most likely be the boss and make the important decisions. What all this shows is that individual personality traits have little impact on the allocation of power in a system as structured as the patriarchy.

Even in societies said to be more advanced in terms of political rights, countries such as Canada and France where equality is legally enshrined, many more men than women hold positions of power in politics, in finance, in cultural industries, in the universities, in religious institutions, in sports, in the military, in the police, even in organized crime, not to mention what we euphemistically call the sex industry. In general, men have more money than women, better jobs with more benefits, and better pensions. Despite the stereotype that women never stop talking, generally it's men who talk more, talk longer, interrupt women, and take control of a conversation. Men usually don't fear being harassed or assaulted by a woman at work or school, in the street, in a bar, or at home. In Canada, men own more than 80 percent of the guns. Men are overwhelmingly the aggressors in cases of spousal and family homicide, as well as in cases of incest (even when the victim is a boy). In short, men generally have more power in society than women.

THOMAS: I had the immense good fortune to witness and participate in two peaceful revolutions. First, the Quiet Revolution in Quebec, where I had a ringside seat because I was teaching during the final years of the classical colleges. I saw a Catholic society rapidly transform itself into a secular society. The second revolution I witnessed was the so-called feminist revolution, which is far from over, where women are beginning to occupy the social position they deserve.

FRANCIS: That's what anarchists—women and men— have been trying to achieve for a long time. Despite all its problems of male domination, misogyny, and even harassment and sexual assault, the anarchist movement since the nineteenth century has been in the vanguard of the struggle for equality of the sexes. Women have been active in union struggles and people's schools to such an extent that anarchists sometimes talk of a "women's rebellion." The 1922 rent strikes in Veracruz, Mexico, for example, were led by the Federation of Libertarian Women, co-founded by María Luisa Marín. Women anarchists have often started their own organizations to circumvent male domination in many anarchist organizations and revolutionary unions. There were the Mujeres Libres during the Spanish Civil War, and the Federation of Women Workers in Bolivia around 1930. Later there was the Centre for Women Anarchists, in Buenos Aires, and the Union of Libertarian Women, in Chile. Mixed-sex organizations, such as the Fédération anarchiste and the Alternative libertaire in France, often have a women's committee or an anti-patriarchy committee to try to counterbalance the male domination and misogyny.

Anarchists have also explored and developed the idea of "free love," the belief that everyone, regardless of sex or orientation, should only enter into a relationship that is fully consensual. Anarchism is often associated with polyamory, the practice of having more than one emotional or sexual relationship at the same time. Love and sexuality should never be subjected to a higher authority, whether religious or state. Anarchists are therefore opposed to marriage, and think it's absurd to promise to love someone forever.

That's the ideal, anyway. In practice, anarchists understand the power of socialization and the patriarchy. They know it's very hard to live consistently and honestly according to one's principles. Some women anarchists have practiced free love, Emma Goldman for example, but historically and in anarchist networks today what seems to happen is that men impose their desires on women. They take more lovers without always being honest and open about it, often without sharing the responsibility for the consequences or even for contraception. And sometimes the person with multiple lovers suddenly becomes jealous when his or her partner has a new affair.

Some anarcha-feminists have come to the conclusion that women lose out far too often in polyamory, owing to differences in socialization between men and women, the de facto inequality between the sexes (even among anarchists), and the presence of "bourgeois" feelings such as jealousy. For that reason, many anarchists prefer to have just one relationship at a time. Obviously, this relationship must be mutually agreed to, free, egalitarian, and revocable at any time. In love as in sex, the principle of voluntary association must prevail.

That's the conclusion Noe Itō arrived at, based on her personal experience. Itō was an early twentieth-century Japanese anarcha-feminist. She called herself an "egoist," i.e., an individualist, but she worked closely with some anarcho-syndicalists. Initially, she advocated the freedom to choose one's marriage partner. Later she rejected the idea of marriage and practiced polyamory instead. But she claimed that there was no equality in her relationship with the anarchist firebrand Ōsugi Sakae. That led her to opt for free and serial monogamy: having many relationships during her lifetime, but one after the other. She wanted her partner to consider her first as a political comrade, next as a friend, and only lastly as a spouse. Itō and Ōsugi were strangled to death in police cells in Japan in 1923.

When these kinds of choices about love and sex become ideological it can create problems in a relationship. For example, a man dogmatically insisting on polyamory might try to impose the lifestyle on his partners, even though they don't want it. The man might accuse his partner of trying to impose monogamy on him, and dismiss monogamy as antithetical to anarchism. Negotiating all this is not easy, especially when a patriarchal (and capitalist) society inculcates in us simplistic notions of love and sexual desire: men are encouraged to be selfish (our desires and pleasures take precedence); women are encouraged to sacrifice (they have to know how to arouse a man, and please him). That's why discussion is so important—to talk as well as to listen—and remembering the principles of freedom, equality, and mutual aid, which presuppose concern for the other's feelings.

A few anarchists go so far as choosing not to have sex, because they don't want to be dominant (for men) or be dominated (for women). Anarchists call this "asexuality." But this is rare.

Obviously, anarchists can change from one type of practice to another over the course of a lifetime.

Capitalism and Employers

THOMAS: Let's move on from the patriarchy to employers, and look at the authority they wield in the workplace. We could go all the way back to slavery, then talk about strikes during the Industrial Revolution and Marx's analysis of the exploitation of workers. But when I look at the world today, I see that some timeless ways of exploiting labour are still with us.

FRANCIS: Didn't you help start a union back in the 1960s?

THOMAS: Yes. In the classical colleges in Quebec there were more laypersons teaching than priests and nuns, so we formed a union, l'Association des professeurs laïques de l'enseignement classique (Association of lay teachers in classical colleges), to fight for better working conditions.

FRANCIS: Unions are generally the best guarantors of better working conditions. But after the Second World War, unions entered into a social contract with the welfare state. They agreed to renounce their combativeness in exchange for benefits, such as paid sick leave and unemployment insurance. In the nineteenth and early twentieth centuries, unions were a major insurrectionary force, in which anarchists could put their principles into practice. But those days are gone. The waning of anarchism may in part be due to the enormous influence of moderate, reformist unions among the working class. In most countries today, the most influential unions are no longer the revolutionary ones. Today's unions are no longer able to carry out autonomous actions, and union leaders thwart the radicalism of grassroots members.

THOMAS: So much has been happening in recent years: jobs have been moved to other countries, workers have been laid off, and salaries have been driven down. The employer has become king and boss, and ordinary workers no longer have any power, not even the power to negotiate. The world of work is a hierarchical world, and authority will never be defeated by replacing one authority with another. So, is it possible for an ordinary worker, an employee, to be an anarchist?

FRANCIS: Many anarchists consider capitalism to be the worst form of domination and exploitation. Marxists say the same. Even liberal philosophers such as Adam Smith say that ultimately, the state is nothing more than a secondary institution whose primary function is to protect the bourgeoisie and private property. In the late nineteenth century, anarchists argued that capitalism, and the poverty it creates, was the primary cause of hunger, begging, vagrancy, theft, murder, prostitution, alcoholism, depression, and suicide.

This idea was enshrined in the Pittsburgh Proclamation, adopted on October 14, 1883 by the founding congress of the International Working People's Association, which included anarchists. It shows up several years later in the manifesto of the Junta Organizadora del Partido Liberal Mexicano, a radical, anarchist-friendly offshoot from the Mexican Liberal Party; Enrique and Ricardo Flores Magón helped found both of those parties.

In 2005 I met an anarchist in Strasbourg who explained his rage against capitalism this way:

> I've worked in bars, on construction sites, in factories, and I tell you, the boss's interests and my interests were completely different. There's a real social war going on: the people close to me—my parents and friends—they're suffering. It's always the same people who are the victims, day after day, in the workplace.

He went on to say: "The only thing capitalism produces are reasons for rebelling against it. All capitalist production creates suffering."

Anarchists have written many books describing the bourgeoisie as a class that lives by exploiting other people's work, and which produces nothing by itself. Louise Michel called the bourgeoisie a parasitic class that feeds on the blood of others, like a "vampire." She said, "Capitalism is a fiction, because it cannot exist without work," adding that "the bourgeois live sumptuously without doing anything." Kropotkin said: "The origin of the wealth of the rich is your misery." Other nineteenth century anarchists described the bourgeoisie and employers as "takers" and anarchists as "sharers." The rich are parasites. As employers they own the means of production, forcing others to sell their time and labour in order to survive. The anarchist Charlotte Wilson defined capitalist "property" as "the domination of an individual, or a coalition of individuals over things.... Property means the monopoly of wealth, the right to prevent others using it, whether the owner needs it or not." Emma Goldman said that private property signified "the dominion of man's needs, the denial of the right to satisfy his needs."

Liberalism is a colossal scam. We claim to live in a democracy and enjoy freedom and equal rights, yet we're obliged to work thirty-five to forty hours a week for more than eleven months a year (in North America) under the authority of a boss who decides what time we get up, how we dress, what time we eat, when, how, and to whom we can talk, and sometimes even when we can go to the toilet. (Thank goodness school prepared us for this!) The boss also decides what work we do, how we do it, what happens to the things we produce, and how the profits of our labour are distributed. The organization of work under capitalism is nothing less than domination and exploitation.

THOMAS: It seems we haven't advanced much beyond the Industrial Revolution and the world of repetitive work depicted in Chaplin's *Modern Times*. We're still being ruthlessly exploited and living under the constant threat of losing our jobs on short notice.

FRANCIS: We're told that that kind of talk is anachronistic—that the world isn't like that anymore, that reality is much more complex, and that social classes no longer exist. In a sense, it's true: today's world is very complex. There's the welfare state, a large middle class, and unions that invest their pension funds in large corporations. But it's also true that vast wealth is still concentrated in the hands of a small number of people who form a class with common interests and who live by dominating and exploiting others. Essentially there are two classes: the bourgeoisie, those men, and more rarely women, who own the large private companies; and the proletariat, those who have no exchange value to offer besides their time and labour. And that's no less true in today's large service companies, which are heavily bureaucratized, than it is in factories.

For anarchists, that state of affairs is unacceptable and revolting. The bourgeoisie are thieves in business suits who live a life of luxury that cannot be sustained without others working to produce surplus. That's the essence of exploitation — to exercise power over others to make them work for you, and to make them work more than they'd have to for their own needs. It's this surplus work that allows the production of wealth. But the wealth doesn't go to those who produce it, instead it goes to the shareholders and the company owners; in other words, the economic elite.

You can't look at the exploitation of an individual in isolation. In principle, I can quit my job, but then I'd have to look for another one, under another boss. Compared with the serfs and slaves of the past, I'm free, but I can only exercise my freedom inside the system: if I refuse to sell my time and labour to any employer, then the bourgeoisie is prepared to let me starve to death. As the German anarchist Erich Mühsam said: "We are fighting for communist anarchy to abolish poverty, not wealth."

THOMAS: Most anarchists come from the dominated class. There are exceptions, but generally that's true. So it's only natural for anarchists to defend the interests of their class.

FRANCIS: Léo Thiers-Vidal, a Belgian anarchist with interesting pro-feminist ideas, said: "The solidarity that I felt with the oppressed, with those who suffered, meant that I spontaneously turned towards anarchism—this theory that addresses relationships of domination."

Kropotkin reproached the science of economics for being obsessed with production and profitability, saying "the only economic science worthy [of] the name [is] a science which might be called 'The Study of the Needs of Humanity, and of the Economic Means to Satisfy Them.'"

Throughout history, anarchists have generally promoted solidarity with the poor and autonomy for workers. Anarchists want to apply the same principles to the economy as to politics; in other words, that no one should be able to impose their will and their standards on the community. Through discussion, the community must collectively decide how to organize itself, how to function, how to work, and how to share the goods they have collectively produced.

Joëlle Zask, a French philosopher (who is not, by the way, an anarchist), has delineated four possible ways to allocate resources within a community: to each a share according to his position or title; to each a share according to his effort or merit; to each a share according to his needs; or to each as much as he wants. Anarchists generally reject the notion of entitlement, whether it's based on nobility, property, sex, or anything else. They also think rewarding effort is a bad idea because some people can't work as much as others, for various reasons (age, sickness, etc.). What's more, some tasks cannot be accomplished in isolation; they require collaboration among people, making it difficult, if not impossible, to distinguish individual contributions. For example, a surgeon cannot successfully carry out a delicate operation unless nurses work alongside him, technicians have correctly sterilized the operating room, and administrative staff have kept good records, ensuring there are stocks of surgical instruments and drugs on hand.

Many tasks rely on the prior accomplishments of others. I can claim that I built a house or wrote a book, but who invented and manufactured the hammer, the saw, and the cement needed to build the house, or the paper, computer, and printing press necessary to produce a book? Who cut the trees to make the lumber or the paper, and who transported all this material? Who made the highway on which the materials were transported? Who produced the food that I ate while building my house or writing my book? Who built the street, and the water and sewage pipes? Who produces the electricity, and who discovered it? All work is collective, in one way or another. You can trace the essential prior work of others back through generations. So, how can we possibly calculate individual contributions when collective work is cumulative?

THOMAS: That's kind of what I was saying at the beginning, with the quote, "We are dwarfs, standing on the shoulders of giants." We should also keep in mind that new jobs are constantly being born, especially in communications, while some traditional jobs are disappearing.

FRANCIS: Yes! It's also important to distinguish between goods that are in abundance and goods that are in shorter supply, as well as between essential and superfluous goods. Who decides on the allocation, in each case? Anarchists have been grappling with these questions for a long time. When circumstances allowed, in communities where the work and the resources were self-managed, anarchists adopted and adapted various ways of distributing resources.

During the Spanish Revolution, the anarchist peasant collective of Alcora allocated goods by family unit, which posed problems for many women who were subject to their husband's authority. Each family had a card entitling it to bread, etc., the card was stamped at the workplace, and each family received the same amount of goods for a day's work, regardless of the kind of work done. Membership of the committee that ran the distribution system changed regularly, to avoid favouritism and bureaucratization.

In another village, Calanda, the community decided that certain scarce goods, such as milk, would be set aside for those with the greatest need — babies, the sick, and the elderly. Other communal goods such as well water and firewood were made available to everyone, and you could take as much as you needed. Obviously there were lazy people in the community; everyone knew who they were. They were scorned, but their needs were still met. Even political adversaries, such as the widows of fascists who had been executed, received their share of the meat. Tobacco was rationed. Alcohol was reserved for the night sentries, to help them keep warm. The community bought two combine harvesters, which were allocated first for use by the community itself, and second for rental to peasants who had refused to join the anarchist collective. After the revolution was defeated and private property was rein- stated, there were more than 130 combine harvesters in the same region; every farmer had one. What a waste of resources!

I know these examples seem to be from another era. Most of us live in big cities, not in peasant communes. But they show that even so-called illiterate peasants caught in a civil war managed to think about anarchist princi- ples and make collective decisions consistent with their ideals. The communities didn't make the same decisions or organize themselves in the same way. That's perfectly normal. Many communities today claim to practice lib- eralism, politically and economically, but they don't all organize themselves in the same way. Different liberal states have different systems of government (presidential vs. constitutional monarchy; two chambers of representa- tives vs. one) and different voting systems (proportional representation vs. first-past-the post; one round of voting or two). Private companies also function in a variety of ways. In a similar vein, the expression of anarchy varies in different contexts, and can reorganize or restructure itself depending on the situation.

THOMAS: You've spoken passionately about capitalism and money. But alongside the real economy there now exists a virtual economy that is a long way from the world of Marx and his exploited workers. Like it or not, how well people live today no longer depends on the "qual- ity" of their work but on factors over which they have no control. Someone sneezes when the stock market opens

in Hong Kong and share prices tumble in New York a
few hours later. Even states have credit ratings now, set by
rating agencies. How can we hope to redistribute wealth
when it is virtual? How do we revolt against a bank that
holds our money and makes billions in profit but gives us
nothing? How do we fight unemployment? The golden
calf is still standing, but instead of four legs it now has a
thousand. What can we actually do to change the system?
Who or what do we target? Everyone agrees that money
dominates the world and that capitalism is out of control.
But throwing a brick through a bank window seems to me
rather pathetic.

FRANCIS: You paint a bleak picture, though you're absolutely right. Let me start with the last thing you said. Since
the alter-globalization movement began staging massive
protests at summit meetings, such as the World Trade
Organization in Seattle in 1999, the G8 in Genoa in 2001,
and the G20 in Toronto in 2010, anarchists have been seen
as the troublemakers who delight in rioting and smashing
the windows of banks and multinational corporations like
McDonald's. There's nothing very revolutionary about
breaking windows, and no one imagines for a minute that
doing so will disrupt the functioning of capitalism, or even
the summits themselves.

The authorities label these acts "violent," but they are
above all symbolic, an expression of rage against the system. They transform political thought into direct action.
There's a good reason why this kind of action, usually
associated with the Black Blocs, has spread so rapidly.
People feel a need to put their radical critique of the

system into practice, and shine a public spotlight on it. It's simply activist tactics.

You asked how to defeat capitalism, what global strategy to adopt. I don't have the answer. And I don't think most anarchists do either. I remember a fascinating discussion I had a few years ago with a Maoist activist who reproached anarchists for not having a strategy. She said she liked the Maoists because they had one. Curious, I asked her what this strategy was. She answered: "Revolution!" But revolution isn't a strategy, it's an end. The strategic question remains: How do we bring about revolution? What organizations do we form? How do we mobilize people? What actions do we take? And what do we do once the revolution is over and capitalism has been overthrown?

If you look through anarchist publications of the last few decades, you'll notice that there are few books and essays about the economy, and few proposals about how to reorganize society economically in line with anarchist principles. It's easier to write about different ways of organizing small groups, as I do, or to denounce elections, capitalism, police repression, prisons, racism, and sexism. There are almost no anarchist analyses of financial capitalism, currency markets, or the banking system.

In the real economy, it's fairly easy to start a restaurant that's self-managed by the employees. But that does nothing to address the problems created by currency speculators and the global movement of capital. Nor does a small business run on anarchist principles solve the problem of a middle class burdened with debt who pay staggering amounts of interest every month to banks and their shareholders. In Canada, for example, a rich country by any standard, more than half the population is still in debt to banks and credit card companies when they retire. Even after a full working life, they are still pouring money into the financial system. The process begins with student debt, which now averages tens of thousands of dollars per graduate in North America. Even before graduating, young people are heavily in debt, which means they have to adjust their lives and aspirations as a consequence: they have to settle down sooner and work more, all in order to pay the financial system. The way the banks exploit us is very different from the way employers exploit us; it's more abstract, though it's no less real.

Debt has often been the trigger for popular revolts, especially in the days when you could be thrown in prison or enslaved for failing to pay a creditor. For example, after the American War of Independence, discharged American soldiers were in such dire financial circumstances that some of them formed militias, burned down courthouses, and attacked prisons to free debtors. The Black Blocs are operating in a long tradition of economic confrontation when they smash bank windows. But to keep things from getting out of hand we don't imprison debtors anymore, we just offer them another credit card.

As if the capitalist system shackling us with debt isn't bad enough, the state imposes taxes on its citizens, forcing us to pay the salaries of the state's civil servants, including me. Obviously I pay income tax too, which is absurd because my salary as a professor at a public university comes from the state; to avoid a lot of administrative work I could simply receive a lower salary and not pay income tax, though my fellow citizens might consider that unfair. And let's not forget all the other forms of economic exploitation in the world today—serfdom, slavery (which still exists), sexual exploitation, and the unpaid domestic and parenting work done by women. They're all part of transnational capitalism.

THOMAS: So is volunteering, as I mentioned before. You can look at it as a form of exploitation by the state, even when it's done in good faith and for a good cause.

FRANCIS: To a certain extent that's true. The global economy is complex, and I don't claim to be able to explain it. Nor will I be so pretentious as to predict the imminent collapse of global capitalism, let alone how it will collapse or what will replace it.

What to do about capitalism and money is a major issue for anarchists. Anarchists are wary of wealth and scorn it outright. They find it distressing that the value of almost everything these days is calculated in terms of money—education, the environment, even sexuality (think of pornography and prostitution). Many anarchists refuse to work. Instead, they salvage edible food thrown away by supermarkets. They try to consume less and exchange more. They try to create and attend low-cost events, like music concerts that are free or by donation. This is not a direct threat to the capitalist system, but it does offer an alternative way of consuming.

THOMAS: Do we need to go back to some form of communism? I know anarchists think communism should be egalitarian, but every country that tried communism in the twentieth century became highly authoritarian — the Soviet Union, China, Cuba, North Korea.

FRANCIS: Unfortunately, those states discredited the communist ideal of a world in which resources and power are shared by everyone. And that's the essence of anarchism — pooling resources, sharing tasks, and making decisions collectively.

Anarchists have been challenging authoritarian statist communists since the nineteenth century. During the First International, Bakunin and Marx clashed over their respective visions for communism and how best to achieve it. Marx and his followers insisted that a revolutionary political party must lead the workers, whereas Bakunin preached grassroots organization through autonomous, revolutionary unions. The anarchists also rejected the idea of taking control of the state through elections. But the Marxists prevailed and Bakunin and his followers were forced out. Marx called Bakunin a "clown," a "schemer," an "opportunist," and a "damn Muscovite." When the anarchists tried to return to the International, during a congress in London in 1896, Jean Jaurès rushed to the podium shouting "No anarchist theories allowed here!" One of Marx's daughters, Eleanor Aveling, declared, "All anarchists are crazy."

Let me quickly outline the basic differences between anarchists and Marxists. Both want to abolish the state. Anarchists want that to happen as quickly as possible. Marxists think it's possible to use the state to abolish capitalism, and that once the bourgeoisie are defeated the state will dissolve by itself. Anarchists don't want any political party. They especially don't want party leaders telling the grassroots revolutionary movement how to seize power. Marxists insist that communist parties must organize and lead the proletariat. Once the revolution has been accomplished, anarchists want self-management and a federation of communes or autonomous unions. Marxists say the state should nationalize the means of production and create workers's councils ("soviets") that follow orders from the revolutionary high command.

Marxist-Leninists claim that history proves Marx was right, since communist revolutions succeeded in Russia, China, Cuba, and elsewhere, whereas all anarchist revolutions have been defeated. But anarchists say there is no point in revolution if it installs an authoritarian or totalitarian regime. It's quite amazing, really: anarchist writers predicted what would happen to authoritarian communism decades before the collapse of the Soviet Union. Bakunin, for example, foresaw that "the State having become sole proprietor . . . will be also the only Capitalist, banker, money-lender, organizer, director of all national labor and distributor of its products. Such is the ideal, the fundamental principle of modern Communism." He went on to say:

> In the People's State of Marx . . . there will . . . be no longer any privileged class, but there will be a government, and, note this well, an extremely complex government, which will not content itself with governing and administrating the masses politically, as all governments do today, but which will also administer them economically,

concentrating in its own hands the production and the just division of wealth, the cultivation of land, the establishment and development of factories, the organization and direction of commerce, finally the application of capital to production by the only banker, the State.

The problem, which anarchists predicted, was that the leaders of the revolutionary party would become a dominant and oppressive ruling elite. Even those party leaders who had been workers would lose touch with the masses and look down on the proletariat from the commanding heights of the state. They would cease to represent the people, and henceforth represent only themselves and the interests of the state. In short, they would become the new "government aristocracy." Marxists were convinced that this dictatorship wouldn't last long, but Bakunin warned that the ultimate goal of every dictatorship is to last as long as possible.

THOMAS: What even the anarchists didn't foresee were the horrendous abuses and massacres that this new ruling class inflicted on their populations. Even after the evidence emerged, many intellectuals sympathetic to communism were slow to acknowledge the truth.

FRANCIS: Nevertheless, apart from the reactionary anti-communist forces, anarchists were the first to criticize the new Bolshevik government after the 1917 Russian Revolution. Anarchists took part in that revolution, but once it succeeded they quickly denounced the political manoeuvring of the Bolsheviks and the massacres they carried out against their former allies, including the anarchists. The Russian anarchist known as Voline, for one, described the new communist state as an "immense bureaucratic apparatus. It ended by forming a widespread and powerful caste of 'responsible' functionaries, which today constitutes a highly privileged stratum." Voline said the party functionaries had become one of the most privileged social classes in the new Russia, especially the "top bureaucracy" that "commands, dictates, orders, prescribes, supervises, punishes. And the middle and even the petty bureaucracy also command and administer, each functionary being master in the sphere assigned to him."

Voline and his anarchist contemporaries, including Emma Goldman and Alexander Berkman, watched the Bolshevik state metamorphose into a deadly monster that turned against anarchism. (Remember the Red Army's brutal repression of the Kronstadt rebellion in 1921.) Nevertheless, many anarchists decided to participate in the new regime, some because they had abandoned their principles, others because they believed the Bolsheviks were right, and still others out of fear for their lives.

The twentieth century demonstrated conclusively that state communism is authoritarian and oppressive—look at the Soviet Union, China, North Korea, and Cuba. Of course, there were gains in education, health, and housing for the people in these countries. But the workplace was never free. Every factory in the Soviet Union was run by a Communist Party appointee, and kept under close surveillance by a political commissar who was also a party appointee. The local trade union was also run by a party member. Together, the factory boss, the commissar, and the union leader ensured that the workers met five-year production targets set by the Minister of Industry. Eventually, Soviet workers formed their own autonomous organizations to protest high work quotas and to demand better wages and working conditions. One of my colleagues at Université du Québec à Montréal, the political scientist Mark-David Mandel, was active for many years in helping form independent trade unions in Russia, Belarus, and elsewhere.

Marxist–Leninist theory maintained that the communist state would dissolve by itself once communism was well established, but the exact opposite happened. A highly authoritarian state clung to power. Even when a centrally planned economy was gradually abandoned in favour of a free market, as in China, the state remained very authoritarian. The predictions of the anarchists have proven accurate.

Racism and Nationalism

THOMAS: We've covered a lot of ground already—the authority of parents, the state, religion, patriarchy, employers, and money. Let's move on now to racism. Each of us is born in a specific place at a specific time. People born somewhere else are different, and it's easy to see them as "the other" and somehow inferior. Of course, those "others" see us as different, too. How many times have I heard someone say, "I'm not racist, *but...*" Racism can take many forms: visible racism, based on skin colour; auditory racism, based on language and accent; cultural racism, based on how a society operates; religious racism, based on faith. As Daniel Sibony wrote in *Le "Racisme," une haine identitaire* ("Racism," an identity hatred):

> Racist theories disparage the "other." For example, the "fact" that blacks are an inferior race justifies their enslavement. But if so much effort is required to put the "other" down, it's because the risk of seeing them rise is high; then it's "us" who would be inferior. The Nazis formulated this ambivalence well: the Jews are the lowest of the low, but at any moment they could rise to the highest positions.

Racism fuels endless conflict by establishing a false hierarchy between individuals, ethnic groups, races, and nations. Essentially, the racist argument is this: if we don't want to be dominated by the "other" we must impose our own dominance. What will it be, our authority or the other's? Anarchists advocate solidarity, mutual aid, and equality, so I assume they're opposed to racism in all its forms.

FRANCIS: Most anarchists think of themselves as global citizens, and are hostile to nationalism. Many actively support immigrants and refugees, who are the victims of racist immigration policies, and physically confront neo-Nazis who threaten or attack immigrants. There are many anarchists in the ranks of protest groups such as Action Antiracist, No Borders, No Person Is Illegal, and Solidarity Across Borders.

Anarchists equate nationalism with militarism and racism. Charles Boussinot, writing in the *Encyclopédie anarchiste*, pointed out the arbitrary nature of nationality:

"Would someone be a Muslim if, instead of being born on the edge of the desert, he was born in the mountains of Scotland, and would you be Catholic if you took your first steps on the plains of the Amur River?" Emma Goldman once asked:

> What is patriotism? Is it love of one's birthplace, the place of childhood's recollections and hopes, dreams and aspirations? ... If that were patriotism, few American men of today would be called upon to be patriotic, since the place of play has been turned into factory, mill, and mine, while [the] deepening sounds of machinery have replaced the music of the birds.

Although where we are born is random, from that moment on we grow up in a society and a culture that inculcate us with the values and norms of the community. Boussinot said cultural identity is "a kind of community of ideas, feelings, tastes, [and] mores which determine how we live together." What, he asked ironically, is "the communion of ideas between Catholics and Protestants? Do clergy and free-thinkers share the same feelings? Nationalists and communists? ... Do peasants and city-dwellers share the same mores? Clergymen and prostitutes? Capitalists and workers?" In a society of unequal systems and opposing classes of interest, attempts to conjure up a national interest or a national identity are pernicious.

THOMAS: Good point. But ultimately aren't we indelibly marked by our childhood memories, by the place and the atmosphere where we grew up? If we move to another country, can we ever fully integrate? And what does that say about those who are forced into exile by economic necessity or political conviction?

FRANCIS: Emma Goldman emigrated from Russia to the United States. She strongly identified with her new chosen country, but not with all of the American people:

> As for myself, in the deeper significance of spiritual values, I feel the United States [is] "my country." Not, to be sure, the United States of the Ku Kluxers, of moral censors in and out of office, of the suppressionists and reactionaries of every type. Not the America of Tammany or of Congress, of respectable inanity, of the highest skyscrapers and fattest moneybags. Not the United States of petty provincialism, narrow nationalism, vain materialism and naive exaggeration. There is fortunately another United States.... The country of Young America of life and thought, or of art and letters; the America of the new generation knocking at the door, of men and women with ideals, with aspirations for a better day; the America of social rebellion and spiritual promise, of the glorious "undesirables" against whom all the exile, expatriation and deportation laws are aimed.

Anarchists in other countries, France for one, should pause to reflect on Goldman's words. So many anarchists claim to be against nationalism, but hold stereotypical and racist ideas about the United States. They say they never want to set foot there because it's full of capitalists, warmongers, and racists. As if the same wasn't true of France!

THOMAS: But there are two Americas, the America of the Democrats and the America of the Republicans, even if both claim to speak for the same America, the strongest country in the world, and both end their speeches with "God Bless America."

FRANCIS: There is also a vast network of activists and anarchists in the United States, especially in the radical milieus of feminism, environmentalism, and anti-racism.

Anarchists generally defend oppressed peoples who are struggling for national liberation, and support the right of nations to an independent country of their own. Many anarchists support Quebec independence, arguing that the Québécois people are unjustly dominated by English Canada. They see popular independence struggles else-where in the world, especially during the 1960s, as good models for Quebec. I used to be a Quebec sovereigntist, but I'm not any more, and I'm not alone in that view. Other anarchists oppose Quebec nationalism but support the liberation struggles of other groups, such as the First Nations and the Palestinians, arguing that in those cases it's more important to oppose the domination, oppression, exploitation, and exclusion than to reject nationalism.

Similarly, anarchists are reluctant to criticize the sex-ism and authoritarianism of Islamic religious elites as long as Islamophobia continues to do so much damage in the West, especially in the United States since 9/11. The West has become obsessed with the "other" (substitute: veiled Muslim women). Anarchists reject the racist rhetoric that sees the West under threat.

The alarmism and victim-playing of conservative dis-course is completely at odds with reality. Conservatives ignore the benefits that immigrants bring to a host society, and the difficulties they face in leaving their country of origin and adapting to a new country. Conservative discourse is blind to the basic sociological and demographic reality: immigrants are a marginalized minority, and the majority population, the "original" people, still control the political, legal, economic, media, scientific, sporting, and cultural institutions, as well as the police, the prisons, and the army.

Many times anarcho-syndicalists have proposed a radical rupture with racist laws in their countries. For example, in the United States in the early twentieth century, when racial segregation was still widespread, the Industrial Workers of the World stated that it was "not a white man's union, not a black man's union, not a red or yellow man's union, but a working man's union." It also said: "We are 'patriotic' for our class, the working class. We realize that as workers we have no country. . . . Our union is open to all workers. Differences of color and language are not obstacles to us."

In Cuba, the anarchist labour organizations Círculo de Trabajadores (Workers' Circle) and the Alianza Obrera (Workers' Alliance) welcomed Spaniards and Cubans of both European and African origin, and protested against racism. During the strike of 1889, workers demanded, among other things, the right to work regardless of skin colour. The following year, during May Day demonstrations, they demanded an end to segregation in Cuba's cafés.

Nationalism is a difficult issue for anarchists, and sometimes provokes sharp debate. On the question of Palestine, for example, some argue that we must support the Palestinian struggle for an independent nation-state, even if the struggle is waged by fundamentalist religious forces who are sexist and homophobic. Others advocate a transnational movement aimed at uniting the Israeli and Palestinian working class. Still others dismiss the term "Palestinian working class" as a euphemism when Palestine is suffering 30 to 50 percent unemployment and its economy is crippled by an Israeli embargo.

With a touch of sarcasm, Uri Gordon, a Jewish–Israeli anarchist, makes the point that no one is really interested in what a few anarchists think about the subject, not in Jerusalem, not in Washington, not at the UN, and not in Palestine. Rather than debating which position is most in accord with abstract anarchist principles, Gordon points to the concrete actions of the collective Anarchists Against the Wall. This Jewish–Israeli group decided to respond directly to calls for help from Palestinian farmers threatened with expropriation of their land by Israel. They met with the farmers, camped on their land, helped with the harvest, and tried to resist expulsion.

Anarchists Against the Wall continue to mobilize, always in response to requests from popular Palestinian movements for demonstrations, blockades, and what they call "unblockading"—sabotaging a roadblock or fence. They have also demonstrated inside Israel against the militarization and colonialism of their country. Though the violence they've faced is much less severe than that meted out to their Palestinian allies, activists from Anarchists Against the Wall have been beaten, arrested, imprisoned, and badly injured. It's the state which attacks them, their own state, which pretends to be defending them against the Palestinians, who in fact are their friends and allies.

By engaging in concrete acts of political solidarity without getting bogged down in abstract debates about principles, Anarchists Against the Wall is a good example of how anarchist citizens of the world can express solidarity.

The Future

THOMAS: There's something I'm still not clear about. We've defined anarchy as the absence of authority, and we've pretty much covered the different forms of authority that anarchists oppose. But *everything* that restricts our freedom is a form of authority. Trying to defeat authority once and for all seems to me to be an endless task: we'd have to be eternal anarchists, continually challenging and rejecting authority. What I haven't heard from you is a clear explanation of *why* we should do that, and *how*.

FRANCIS: Well, you can look at anarchism as a process, an endless and continuously evolving journey towards an ideal state of anarchy. Anarchists are constantly debating the language, organization, and practice of anarchy, and criticizing some of their allies for not being sufficiently anti-authoritarian.

THOMAS: I think what's changed is not so much the meaning of the word *authority*, but how it's used. Authority isn't what it used to be. Targeting a dictator or king is clear and easy to understand: you attack the supreme authority in order to overthrow it. But how do you attack something as nebulous as the state, or a religion, or employers, or capitalism, or racism? Who actually holds the authority? Who represents it?

It's easy to be outraged these days; just open a newspaper or listen to the news. We all want to change things, but how do we go from outrage to action? My impression is that most people don't want to destroy authority, they just want to replace one authority with another. So, here's one of my last questions: do anarchists have a role in the future?

FRANCIS: Well, as the anarchists battling the police and austerity politics in Greece say, "We are an image of the future!" But I understand your pessimism, or perhaps it's realism, when you say that most people just want to replace one authority with another. This takes us back to the notion of voluntary servitude. The French sociologist Béatrice Hibou talks about the "desire for the State," even among people who live under authoritarian regimes. Low-wage workers often show deference to their bosses, and some abused women forgive their violent partners rather than leave the relationship. Domination, oppression, and inequality are toxins that pollute our psyche and our social relations, muddy our conscience, and undermine our self-esteem. They make it hard for us to imagine another kind of life, to imagine rebelling in order to be free, individually and collectively.

But I also know, as Kropotkin said:

At all times beginning with Ancient Greece, there were persons and popular movements that aimed, not at the

substitution of one government for another, but at the
abolition of authority altogether. They proclaimed the
supreme rights of the individual and the people, and
endeavoured to free popular institutions from forces
which were foreign and harmful to them, in order that
the unhampered creative genius of the people might
remould these institutions in accordance with the new
requirements.

Kropotkin and his friend Élisée Reclus believed that
anarchy and modern science would come together for the
common good, and that the twentieth century would be
the century of anarchism.

Obviously they were wrong, and it's easy to dismiss
their optimism as naive, given the strength of the state and
capitalism in the twenty-first century. But imagine what
an anarchist transported from the late nineteenth century, someone who was active in the revolutionary trade
unions in Paris, for example, would find in many countries
today: Child labour abolished. Coeducation the norm and
schools accessible to everyone. No compulsory military
service. No death penalty. Women equal under the law to
men (even if they aren't always equal in practice). Legal
contraception and abortion. Legal homosexuality and gay
marriage. Widespread vegetarianism. Nudism allowed in
some places. Workers with the right to meet, form unions,
and go on strike. An eight-hour work day, a thirty-five to
forty-hour week. Paid vacation days and paid sick days.
Public insurance programs for injured and unemployed
workers. Freedom of thought and freedom of speech,
both protected by law.

"This is anarchy!" our time-travelling militant would exclaim — until he or she noticed the strength of the state and its police and armies, the persistence of racism and patriarchy, the power of capitalism and the financial system, and the strength and arrogance of employers, who are only mildly inconvenienced by changes in the law.

THOMAS: Can anarchists take sole credit for all those advances in society?

FRANCIS: No, of course not, but anarchists were almost the only ones fighting for those rights during the middle and late nineteenth century, and were persecuted as a result. At the time, people considered anarchist goals and ideas childish, absurd, and dangerous.

Increasingly I see anarchist principles and practices being incorporated into all kinds of activist networks. The police, politicians, and media have all been talking about a revival of anarchism, especially since the Zapatista uprising in Chiapas, Mexico, in 1994, and the emergence of the alter-globalization movement in the late 1990s. Anarchism has strongly influenced the anti-austerity movement that arose after the financial crisis of 2008. Both the Indignados movement in Spain and the international Occupy movement of 2011, with its slogan "We are the 99 percent against the 1 percent!" were essentially anarchist. Occupy didn't claim to be anarchist, and its discourse was naive and often incoherent, but the hundreds of self-managed camps set up in cities around the world and the experimentation with participatory democracy were essentially anarchist in practice.

Anarchists were a major force in the longest student strike in Quebec history, in 2012. Germany and Greece have the strongest and best organized anarchist networks today, and thousands of anarchists take to the streets in those countries in demonstrations. Granted, it's a far cry from Spain in the 1930s, when hundreds of thousands of anarchists, many of them armed, ran the factories, businesses, and peasant communes.

Anarchism is incarnate in the organization of militant groups when they function without leaders and arrive at decisions by consensus, whether in a small collective or a large popular assembly. Anarchy is incarnate in the actions of militant groups when people act autonomously and at the same time in solidarity with one another, without leaders telling them where to march, what to think, or what strategy to follow. Anarchy finds its voice in songs, in cyberspace, in protest marches. Anarchy is expressed every time someone waves a black flag in the street, or paints a circle–A on a wall somewhere. Anarchy can flower in social movements—in ways of organizing and decision-making, in the language of signs, banners and slogans, and in street demonstrations. Anarchy expresses itself in acts of solidarity with people who are not necessarily anarchists—refugees threatened with expulsion, for example, or aboriginal communities.

THOMAS: All this leaves me wondering whether anarchist actions and protests serve any purpose in the end. Do anarchists have any influence on the evolution of society, or does society only change when enough individuals recognize the need to alleviate injustices and inequalities?

FRANCIS: Randall Amster, an American anarchist, tried to evaluate the effectiveness and impact of anarchism today. He concluded that conventional methods to evaluate the effectiveness of an ideology or social movement could not be applied to anarchism. What purpose would it serve, he asked, to know the impact of anarchism on political parties or election results? Why try to convince the mass media to portray anarchists in a positive light?

It's just as difficult to know whether anarchists have had any influence on specific legal reforms or on national or international politics. Amster says it would be much more interesting to know whether anarchism, as a political philosophy, ideology, and social movement, encourages people to explore new ways of living, collectively and individually. But where, he asks, do we look for evidence of this happening: in society in general, in public and private institutions, in militant anarchist networks, or in the personal relationships of anarchists?

THOMAS: Surely that's a question of the *modus operandi* of anarchists, the actions they take, rather than the reasons for their actions. But why challenge authority? Because it bothers you? Because it stifles freedom? Because inequality will never end as long as society is dominated by an authority? And how do we actually eradicate authority and establish an egalitarian or anarchist society?

FRANCIS: I think I've already suggested the reasons why anarchists want to topple authority. But how do we actually establish an anarchist society? Some anarchists advocate a kind of anarcho-reformism, working within the system to

promote more freedom, equality, and political participation in existing institutions like school boards, municipal
councils, and unions. The French sociologist Philippe
Corcuff, who migrated ideologically from Trotskyism to
anarchism, suggests something called "social-democratic
libertarianism." He advocates developing autonomous,
self-managed spaces while at the same time defending the
social services provided by the welfare state.

Paul Goodman, in the United States, and Colin
Ward, in Britain, both support this approach. Ward,
who died in 2010, became an anarchist while doing his
military service in Britain in the 1940s. In the 1960s, he
participated in a debate started by George Molnar in two
journals called *Freedom* and *Anarchy*. Molnar maintained
that it made no sense to think of establishing an anarchist society, because there would always be resistance
to anarchism and it went against the very principles of
anarchism to impose one's will through domination or
coercion. Thus it would be absurd to think of anarchism
as a plan for a completely anarchist society. Molnar said
that anarchism must be simultaneously positive and negative: anarchists must be in "permanent opposition" to all
forms of authority (the critical, or negative aspect), but
at the same time individual anarchists must assert their
freedom "here and now" (the programmatic, or positive
aspect).

THOMAS: So is the debate essentially a choice between
individual anarchism, a kind of permanent protest against
any form of authority, and collective anarchism, which
would be the only way to start a revolution?

FRANCIS: No, it's a question of figuring out the best way
for anarchism and anarchists to have an impact, however
limited, in today's society. Andy Chan, an academic, interviewed twenty-odd anarchists in the early 1990s. A few
expected to see a revolution in their lifetime, in the wake
of an economic, environmental, or nuclear crisis, but only
two said the goal of their activism was revolution. The
overwhelming majority didn't see any revolution on the
horizon. Their political activism had more modest and
realistic goals. These included publicly challenging and
resisting the state and capitalism; encouraging radical
critical thinking in the face of the state and capitalism;
informing people about anarchism; and expanding activist
networks.

Colin Ward didn't believe revolution was possible
either, but he was wary of the purely critical, individu-
alistic anarchism of "permanent opposition." Ward tried
to define a middle position for anarchism as a revolutionary force. He admired the workers' movement of the
nineteenth century, before the birth of the welfare state.
Workers then practiced mutual aid by helping one another
during times of unemployment, sickness, accident, and
death (taking care of orphaned children, for example).
And they established centres where workers could meet
and if necessary borrow money, at no interest, from a
common fund.

Ward saw the birth of the welfare state after the
Second World War as a catastrophe. He claimed that
state-administered welfare destroyed autonomous,
organic networks of mutual aid, especially within the
working class. It fostered dependence on the state, and

allowed public agencies to discipline, control, and suppress welfare recipients. Ultimately, what interested Ward
were not just anarchist organizations, but all individual
and group strategies for mutual aid, even those that didn't
call themselves anarchist. Ward believed they all helped
create "pockets of anarchy" in the world. Some people use
the terms "micro-revolutions" or "here and now" anarchy
to describe these attempts to create free moments and
spaces.

Ward says pockets of anarchy are possible when people
are committed to practicing autonomy and mutual aid. If
they're to respect the spirit of anarchy, the organizations
that emerge must be voluntary (you can join and leave at
will), practical (dealing with concrete problems), temporary (to avoid the fossilization and power games that come
with the rise of an elite), and small scale (so people can
meet face to face). Marginalized and self-marginalizing
people, such as homeless people or punks, can form
networks that are essentially anarchist, despite the fre-
quent violence and misery of their lives. Thus a society
can be partly anarchist, a work-in-progress. Ward says
it's important to act in the present moment with specific
conditions, addressing housing problems, for example, or
starting community gardens.

At the heart of the matter are relationships between
individuals and between groups: we need to encourage
changes in attitudes and practices, and create new institutions to foster individual and collective autonomy. We also
need to look for ways to support existing pockets of anarchy in society, those groups of people who have decided
among themselves, autonomously and without a leader,

what they want to do and how they want to act, people
who want to practice mutual aid in a self-governing, free,
and egalitarian manner.

Personally, I share Ward's belief that anarchism can
influence society and institutions gradually, that it can
be reformist, so to speak, and that it's always possible
to carve out more space for freedom and equality. But I
also strongly believe that anarchism must be more than
reformist; it shouldn't just be reasonable and moderate.
Elun Gabriel, a historian who studied the influence of
anarchist propaganda on German socialism around 1900,
rightly observed that it's the radical and irreverent side
of anarchism that is the most important. The socialist
leaders of the time were becoming increasingly reformist, but the German workers, who usually voted socialist,
were inspired by anarchist newspapers to demand a more
radical approach. The newspapers offered exhilarating
hope of a new and completely different society, and were
scathing in their critique of the authoritarian socialist elite
and its moderate approach.

So I believe that anarchism should not just be reformist, content with improving the existing system and creating spaces for more freedom, equality, and mutual aid.
We must continue to insist that the state, the patriarchy,
capitalism, and racism are wholly illegitimate and unjust
systems. They must be fought and eradicated. And that's
why I believe we also need combative forms of anarchism,
such as the Black Blocs, that translate ideas into direct
action. Anarchism should threaten the status quo, for
example by disturbing the decorum of large international
summits. Thirty years ago anarchists had almost no voice,

but today anarchism's radical critique of the state and capitalism is being heard in the media and in cyberspace.

THOMAS: So there's no such thing as a moderate anarchist. When I write a letter to the editor to protest something that I find unjust or which infringes on my liberty, I'm simply a protester, an indignant individual, not a fledgling anarchist, even though I'm being critical of authority.

FRANCIS: The heart of anarchy is a radical critique of the state and capitalism, and therefore a call for revolution to destroy those systems. Anarchism takes inspiration from the great anarchist revolutionary moments—the Paris Commune, the Spanish Civil War, May '68. But how do we create these moments? The answer is not, as republicans or Marxist–Leninists advocate, to take control of parliament. To have an anarchist revolution, the people themselves must take charge.

Throughout history, every anarchist revolution has ended in massacres and the imposition of new authoritarian regimes—republican after the Paris Commune, Marxist–Leninist after the Russian revolution, fascist in Spain in 1939. The French anarchist author Michel Ragon titled one of his novels *La Mémoire des vaincus* (Memory of the defeated). That might sound disheartening, but does it mean that anarchists are wrong? I don't believe so. I'd be much more disheartened if I thought the only freedom possible was that offered by liberalism or capitalism, because they are simply incapable of eradicating the great political and economic inequalities of our times. I don't

know if I'll witness a revolution in my lifetime. Most of
the time I doubt it. And I fear that if a revolution does
happen it will bring evil and disappointment, and in the
end, not much anarchy.

Even if I don't have much hope of seeing anarchy triumph in my lifetime, it doesn't stop me. Hope of a better
life rouses my anger against unjust systems; that's what
motivates me to keep trying to create spaces for anarchy,
and to keep spreading the word. I'm a "combative pessi-
mist," to revive the name of a 1980s punk radio program
in Paris. Anarchism is a process, a hands-on experience,
a genuine political force. It's a commitment to living and
acting in harmony with anarchist principles, despite the
contradictions within the anarchist movement. Anarchists
live and act in defiance of the powerful systems we're
trying to defeat. Anarchists are outsiders. Society's rules,
norms, and structures are completely irreconcilable with
the anarchist spirit and our vision of a better life.

THOMAS: We've come a long way from my first innocent
question, "What is anarchy?" Your answers have led me
off the beaten path, into terrain I never knew existed. I've
read pamphlets and books I'd never heard of before, and
you've motivated me to think for myself about a lot of
things, not just anarchy. I'm happy to say that I've shed a
lot of my old prejudices about anarchy. I no longer accept
the stereotypical view of anarchism as a negative force,
and see now that it is actually full of hope. Anarchism
aspires to abolish authority, or power, to establish a free
and egalitarian society. Freeing ourselves from parental
authority comes naturally, if we've had a good upbringing.

We can try to free ourselves from the authority of the state by creating systems of mutual aid. To counter the authority of religion, we can insist that it remain in the private domain and that society make space for atheists. To fight the patriarchy we can encourage and support feminism. We can oppose capitalism with mutual aid and by joining the alter-globalization movement. We can fight racism in all its forms by remaining vigilant and deconstructing theories that extol the superiority of one race over another. And when people ask us why we bother, why we carry on this utopian struggle without end, we can answer: to try to achieve a society whose motto could be "Freedom, equality, mutual aid, and justice."

Let's end where we began, but this time with Louise Michel's beautiful definition: "Anarchy is order through harmony." That could serve as an epigraph for this book. But let's also remember what Noam Chomsky said: "No one owns the term 'anarchism.'"

Post-Trump Anarchism

Afterword for the 2017 English translation
Translated by Ellen Warkentin

THOMAS: Like much of the world, I followed the turns taken by the 2016 American presidential race with interest, and like much of the world, I was shocked at Donald Trump's unexpected triumph. It made me seriously question the US electoral system, which is unlike that of any other country. For a nation that sends expert election observers to other countries to ensure that their elections remain democratic, it seems like they should take a close look at their own system.

FRANCIS: As we have already mentioned, anarchists generally choose not to vote, justifying this choice with a number of very defensible rationales: they consider it absurd to choose a master; they feel that voting leads to passivity and reinforces the credibility of a totally illegitimate system, etc. Anarchists have, however, been convinced to vote on rare occasions; for example, when certain candidates were promising to free political prisoners in Spain in the early twentieth century, or in an attempt to block the election of

201

an extreme right-wing politician to the French presidency in 2002 and again in 2017. Some supporters of anarchist politics, including Noam Chomsky, suggest that anarchists should vote for the "least bad" candidate (Green or Democrat), but warn that anarchists must never forget to take action to put pressure on the elected elite. This line of reasoning suggests that as anarchists we must take action, and we can vote, too.

And yet many anarchists, including Voltairine de Cleyre in the United States and Sébastien Faure in France, saw elections not as a positive addition to the political process, but, for reasons already discussed, as a negative distraction. Elections are also an appalling waste of the political energy of tens of thousands of volunteers and hundreds of millions of dollars, resulting in tons of propaganda that will end up in our massive landfills.

Anarchists are often virtuous, moral people. They feel that voting for a particular politician binds you politically and morally to the decisions of that politician, that you share responsibility for their actions—and for their crimes, including any wars they may wage. You think Barack Obama was a nice president. Maybe, but if you voted for him you aren't only supporting his positive achievements; you also share responsibility for his crimes. Obama continued wars in Iraq and Afghanistan and authorized—by his signature—hundreds of drone-strike murders. In the eyes of these anarchists, the people who voted him in are morally and politically complicit in these atrocities.

And yet beyond these general considerations, the 2016 American elections showed once again that the

US electoral system is dysfunctional. Since there is only one president, the winning side automatically takes the presidency—even if they only received 50 percent of the vote. But it's even more ludicrous than that: Trump received the support of only around 20 to 25 percent of American adults, if you take into consideration those who abstained, those who spoiled their ballots, those who voted for Clinton, and those who aren't even registered to vote—a number that includes, in many states, incarcerated people, parolees and ex-cons. And Trump is not an anomaly: American presidents are always voted in by around 25 percent of the electorate. These presidents are elected monarchs, and a very small minority elects them.

THOMAS: Donald Trump has also repeatedly claimed that the electoral system was rigged. Even after his victory, he made a point of contesting the fact that the majority of the popular vote went to Hillary Clinton, and he and his supporters attacked those who protested his election. One of his supporters even declared: "These are communists. These are anarchists. They're anti-Semitic"; "They want to foment anarchy in the United States." There is no doubt: the "red menace" is back, but this time it also flies a black flag.

FRANCIS: It is not new to see anarchists and other radicals participate in more or less turbulent protests after an American election, sometimes even ransacking political party headquarters. The January inauguration ceremony in Washington has often been an occasion to mobilise against a new president. In 1973, protesters against US involvement in Vietnam targeted Richard Nixon. In 2001, thousands showed up to protest the election of George W. Bush, which was tainted by irregularities in Florida. In fact, every political camp has organized protests against a president, depending on who is elected and the issues at hand.

That being said, anarchists believe it is not enough just to protest; we must also organize locally. This was the stated position of the First of May Anarchist Alliance and the Black Rose/Rosa Negra Anarchist Federation immediately following the 2016 election. Anarchists can once again turn to the words of African-American feminist Patricia Hill Collins, who said that a social movement must have a visible face that stages protests, but it must also have a hidden face that works for the survival of organizations, collectives and individuals. This second aspect is essential in periods of social and political backlash, like today, and it is often the work of women.

Trump has announced that he wants to go after illegal immigrants—a population that anarchists often mobilize to support. Anarchist People of Colour (apoc) is particularly involved in this struggle, considering that Trump is notoriously racist. Since he came to power, racist groups and supporters of white supremacy seem to have lost some of their former restraint. For decades now, anarchists have been teaming up with American antiracist and antifascist groups such as the Anti-Racist Action (ara) network and the Antifascist Action groups, known as "antifa." It is therefore no surprise that increasing numbers of protests have been disrupting events and gatherings of racists, sexists, homophobes and transphobes, and that anarchists are a presence at these protests, sometimes taking the shape of Black Blocs and facing the white supremacists head-on.

THOMAS: It is also no surprise to see Trump attacking anarchists and communists. The practice is over a hundred years old in the United States: Congress adopted the Anarchist Exclusion Act in 1903, while the Alien Registration Act, better know as the Smith Act, which targeted communist activists, was passed in 1940.

When you look at the provisions of these two laws, doesn't it seem like there is really nothing new going on here?

FRANCIS: It is true that western nations have long sought to crack down on anarchists (and communists), and have often confused anarchism and immigration — sometimes with just cause, as many anarchists were immigrants. Jews from Eastern Europe, Germans, Italians and Spaniards were among those who came to America in the late nineteenth and early twentieth centuries. Some were anarchists fleeing repression in their home countries, while others became anarchists when they saw the living conditions in the United States, with its long history of capitalistic exploitation and racism. However, back then, violence was rife on both sides of the equation. The state killed off anarchists in labour conflicts or after rushing them through bogus trials, while anarchists planned assassination attempts.

The laws you mentioned directly targeted anarchists, as did the infamous *Lois scélérates* in France and elsewhere in Europe, which made it a crime to possess anarchist literature or promote anarchism. These days, while the anarchist and anti-authoritarian movement has been the object of thousands of arrests at alterglobalization and anti-austerity protests, and while "anti-terrorism" laws give more and more power to the authorities, we are nowhere near the level of violence and repression experienced by anarchists in the early twentieth century.

Today, the state identifies "radical Islam," in both its imported and domestic iterations, as a principal threat. Certainly, the media tries to draw parallels between the anarchist Black Blocs and the Islamic State militias, observing that both groups wear black masks or hoods. President Trump and reactionary and conservative journalists and pundits also equate neo-Nazis with antifascist–anarchists (antifa), claiming there is "violence" on both sides. A more legitimate concern, however, is the appearance of organizations like the Montreal-based Centre for the Prevention of Radicalization Leading to Violence, which monitors Muslim communities, but also keeps an eye on extreme right- and left-wing movements. These organizations define "radicalization" as simply a move toward "violence." They see no difference between launching an attack using firearms (as practiced by certain radical Islamists and anti-abortion activists in the United States), and throwing a rock through the window of a fashionable boutique in a neighbourhood undergoing gentrification (as practiced by certain anarchists). This lack of distinction between the "violence" of anarchists and that of radical Islamists or right-wing neo-Nazis and anti-feminists allows such organizations to exaggerate the anarchist threat to public security, which only facilitates the repression of anarchists by justifying surveillance and infiltration operations, provocation, and preventive arrests.

I want to conclude on a different note, by stating that anarchists are radicals who do not believe in the legitimacy of the justice system, or in God (in principle). Yet anarchists often support people who have been imprisoned without proof on the pretext that they are "radical Islamists." Anarchists are demanding what moderate progressives, or even republicans and liberals, should demand: a fair and equitable hearing according to the principles of the justice system itself, with full knowledge of the evidence collected against the accused, the right to a fair trial, etc. In these times when xenophobia (Islamophobia) and the 'war on terror' dominate the popular imagination, it's often the anarchists—both people of colour and those considered white—who we see standing up for principles that republicans or liberals would consider just. Or defending tolerance and respect for difference, for example of Muslim women wearing hijab. These anarchists are fundamentally atheist, but they stand up to defend Muslim women who wish to express their faith by wearing hijab, because anarchists are on the side of anyone who is the victim of racist hatred. This apparent paradox can be explained by the fact that anarchists adhere to the fundamental values of freedom, equality and solidarity, including the expression of such values in people who are not anarchists; but also because many anarchists often feel like strangers in their own country, and have been direct victims of intolerance and repression.

Notes

See the Bibliography for details of Principal Works Cited.
[Tr. JG] indicates the quotation was translated by John Gilmore for this edition.

p. 5   *I was always for a free republic*   John Adams, letter to Mercy Warren, 30 July 1807. Collections of the Massachusetts Historical Society, vol. 4, fifth series, 1878, p. 394.

5   *Disappear at least, revolting distinctions*   Marechal, *Manifesto of the Equals.*

9   *the condition of a people who*   Anselme Bellegarrigue, "Manifeste de l'Anarchie," *L'anarchie, Journal de l'Ordre,* no. 1, April 1850 [Tr. JG].

9   *from the vantage point of absolute or democratic truth*   Bellegarrigue, *Anarchist Manifesto.*

12   *There's something that astounds me*   Octave Mirbeau, "La grève des électeurs," *Le Figaro,* 28 November 1888, trans. Mitchell Abidor for marxists.org.

16   *As Socialism in general*   Kropotkin, *Modern Science and Anarchism,* chapter 1.

20   *We are not anarchists*   Julieta Paredes (member Mujeres Creando), interviewer and trans. unknown, n.d. Reprinted in *Green Anarchy,* no. 9 (summer 2002): 18.

23   *Anarchism is essentially a state of mind*   Préposiet, *Histoire de l'anarchisme,* 13 [Tr. JG].

27   *The instinct of liberty naturally revolted*   Voltairine de Cleyre, "Why I Am An Anarchist."

29 *To be an anarchist is to deny authority*   Émile Armand, "Mini-Manual
    of Individualist Anarchism." https://theanarchist
    library.org/library/emile-armand-mini-manual-of-
    individualist-anarchism. First published in French in Faure, *L'en-
    cyclopédie anarchiste.*

30 *There were people opposed to power*   Reclus, "L'anarchie" (1894).
    (Paris: Éditions du Sextant, 2006). [Tr. JG].

37 Lahontan, *Dialogues avec un sauvage*, ed. Réal Ouellette (Montreal:
    Lux Éditeur, 2010).

37 *The work of the anarchist*   Émile Armand, "Mini-Manual," part 1.

38 *Kessler's idea was*   Kropotkin, *Mutual Aid*, introduction. http://
    dwardmac.pitzer.edu/Anarchist_Archives/kropotkin/mutaidcontents.
    html

39 *Loye found twenty-four mentions*   Loye, *Darwin's Lost Theory.*

39 *Those communities which included the greatest*   Charles Darwin, *The
    Descent of Man*, 2nd edition (London: H.M. Caldwell, 1874): 163.

41 *what is considered as good among ants*   Kropotkin, *Anarchist Morality*,
    30.

41 *The distinction . . . between egotism*   Kropotkin, ibid., 81, 79, 80.

43 *power makes one ferocious*   Louise Michel, quoted in Marian Leigh-
    ton, "Anarcho-Feminism and Louise Michel," *Our Generation* 21, no.
    2 (summer 1990), 22–29. Also in Black Rose Collective, *Black Rose 1,
    Journal of Contemporary Anarchism* (Los Angeles: Black Rose Collec-
    tive, n.d.): 8–36.

43 *great men have more opportunities*   Reclus, *L'Évolution, la révolution
    et l'idéal anarchique*, 3 [Tr. JG].

43 *from the moment a man*   Ibid., 149.

43 *The best, the purest, the most intelligent*   Bakunin, quoted in Mark
    Leier, *Bakunin*, 184.

43 *Power tends to corrupt*   Lord Acton (John Emerich Edward Dal-
    berg-Acton), Letter to Bishop Mandell Creighton, 5 April 1887, in
    Acton, *Historical Essays and Studies*, eds. J.N. Figgis and R.V. Laurence
    (London: Macmillan, 1907).

43 *Far from living in a world of visions*   Kropotkin, "Anarchism: Its Phi-
    losophy and Ideal," in Baldwin, *Kropotkin's Revolutionary Pamphlets*,
    135.

44 *the employer would never be the tyrant*   Ibid., 135–36.

44 *We have not two measures*   Kropotkin, *Anarchism: A Collection of
    Revolutionary Writings.*

46   *Throughout the history of our civilization*   Kropotkin, *The State.*

47   *for the greater part of humanity*   Sahlins, *The Western Illusion,* 51.

50   *Nature is the sum of all things*   Bakunin, "Considérations philosophiques sur le fantôme divin, le monde réel et l'Homme" (1870–71), in Maximoff, *Political Philosophy of Bakunin,* 53.

52   *Anarchism is a world-concept*   Kropotkin, *Modern Science and Anarchism,* chapter 7.

52   *Evolution is the infinite movement*   Élisée Reclus, *L'évolution, la révolution et l'idéal anarchique* (1898), quoted in Knowles, *Political Economy from Below,* 204.

52   *It's by myriads and myriads that revolutions succeed*   Reclus, *L'Évolution,* 3 [Tr. JG].

53   *Science is an essentially anarchist enterprise*   Feyerabend, *Against Method,* 9.

53   *Anarchism helps*   Ibid., 18.

58   *Anarchist fictions*   Eisenzweig, *Fictions de l'anarchisme.*

59   *The heroes of hell*   Davis, *Les héros de l'enfer.* See also John Wiener, "Mike Davis Talks About 'The Heroes of Hell'," *Radical History Review* no. 85 (winter 2003), 227–38.

62   *Anarchists are not trying to spread fear*   Colson, *Petit lexique,* 325–28.

63   *Anarchism does create rebels*   Goldman, quoted in Glassgold, *Anarchy!,* 23.

63   *I killed the President*   Jeffrey W. Seibert, *I Have Done My Duty: The Complete Story of the Assassination of President McKinley* (Berwyn Heights, MD: Heritage Books, 2002).

63   *The Psychology of Political Violence*   Goldman, "The Psychology of Political Violence" in Goldman, *Anarchism and Other Essays,* 85–114.

63   *Now and After: The ABC of Communist Anarchism*   Berkman, *Now and After.* Reprinted under various titles including *What is Communist Anarchism?* and *What is Anarchism?*

64   *With the poor, always*   Séverine, "Les responsables," *Le Cri du peuple,* 30 January 1887. Quoted in Claude Baudry, "Séverine de son vrai nom Caroline Rémy, insurgée toute sa vie," *L'Humanité,* 9 July 2012 [Tr. JG].

66   *The Many-Headed Hydra*   Suzanne Berger, *Notre première mondialisation: Leçons d'un échec oublié* (Paris: Seuil, 2003). See also: Berger, "Puzzles from the First Globalization" in Miles Kahler and David Lake, eds., *Politics in the New Hard Times: The Great Recession in Comparative Perspective* (Cambridge: Cambridge University Press, 2013): 150–168.

67   *Write an article against this race*   Proudhon, 26 December 1847,
      Carnets (Paris: M. Rivière, 1960), 337–39. Trans. Mitchell Abidor for
      Marxists.org.

72   *To a greater or lesser extent*   Mbah and Igariwey, *African Anarchism*,
      27.

77   *It is not popular to attack Castro in Europe.*   Montseny, quoted in Fer-
      nandez, *Cuban Anarchism*, chapter 5.

85   *Feminism as a whole*   Brown, "Beyond Feminism: Anarchism and
      Human Freedom," in Ehrlich, *Reinventing Anarchy*, 153.

91   *In a 1968 article titled "Poor Black Woman"*   Patricia Robert-
      son, "Poor Black Woman" in *Poor Black Woman* (brochure, various
      authors), (Boston: New England Free Press, 1968): 4.

91   *Do not take liberties with women*   "Rules of the Black Panther Party:
      8 Points of Attention, #7" (Tucson. Arizona: The Sixties Project,
      1993). http://www2.iath.virginia.edu/sixties/HTML_docs/Sixties.
      html

92   *this logical contradiction between revolution and sexism*   Éloise
      Gaudreau, "Interprétations de la tension entre principes de lutte et
      pratique militante en matière de rapports de genre dans les organisa-
      tions libertaires: le cas de l'Union communiste libertaire." Master's
      thesis, Université du Québec à Chicoutimi, 2013.

97   *since it has been demonstrated that property is theft*   Rodolfo Gonzales
      Pacheco, "Robbers." Editorial in *La Antorcha*, 6 May 1921. Quoted in
      Osvaldo Bayer, *The Anarchist Expropriators*. Translated by Paul Shar-
      key. Oakland: AK Press, 2015.

97   *What is Property?*   Proudhon, *What is Property?*

97   *the end of theft eternally committed*   Michel, *Prise de possession*, 62 [Tr.
      JG].

99   *Les Sorcières (The Witches) published an editorial*   Les Sorcières, "On
      prend des risques: Notre position féministe et anarchiste sur l'ex-
      ploitation sexuelle," editorial, *Les Sorcières* 8, no.12 (spring 2012): 2–5
      [Tr. JG]. http://www.lessorcieres.org/journaux.html

106   *I bow before the authority of special men*   Bakunin, *God and the State*,
      chapter 2. http://dwardmac.pitzer.edu/Anarchist_Archives/bakunin/
      godandstate/godandstate_ch1.html#II

110   *for as long as man has thought*   Attali, *Demain*, 11 [Tr. JG].

111   *The reason of those best able*   Jean de La Fontaine, "The Wolf and the
      Lamb," trans. Eli Siegel, in Siegel, *Hail, American Development* (New
      York: Definition Press, 1968).

111   *Which country, coalition, or international organization*   Attali, *Demain*,
      back cover [Tr. JG].

111 *I've had to fight doubly hard*   Shirley Chisholm, quoted in Kira Cochcrane, ed., *Women of the Revolution: Forty Years of Feminism* (New York: Guardian Books, 2010): 10.

115 *Parental authority is a cluster*   French Civil Code (amended 1 July 2013), Art. 371–1, trans. LegiFrance. https://www.legifrance.gouv.fr/Traductions/en-English/Legifrance-translations

117 *A well-trained mind*   Michel de Montaigne, *Essais*, book 1, chapter 26 [Tr. JG].

118 *will no longer be a detested tyrant*   Guillaume, quoted in Avrich, *The Modern School Movement*, 13.

118 *essential to open children's eyes*   Pelloutier, quoted in Jennings, 19.

118 *children will be entirely free*   James Guillaume, "Ideas on Social Organization: IV: G. Education" (1874). https://www.marxists.org/reference/archive/guillaume/works/ideas.htm

119 *government [is] a necessary organ of social life*   Malatesta, *Anarchy* (1891 pamphlet), part 1. https://theanarchistlibrary.org/library/errico-malatesta-anarchy

120 *indigenous anarchism*   Alfred, *Wasase*. See also: Alfred and Gord Hill, "L'anarcho-indigénisme: Entrevues avec Gerald Taiaiake Alfred et Gord Hill," interviewed by Francis Dupuis-Déri and Benjamin Pillet, *Possibles* 23 March 2016; and Alfred, "Interview with Gerald Taiaiake Alfred about Anarchism and Indigenism in North America" (2010), interviewer unknown, Alpine Anarchist Productions. http://www.alpineanarchist.org/r_i_indigenism_english.html

121 *The best way of being free*   Kropotkin, *Words of a Rebel*, chapter 13.

122 *The state is a social relationship*   Landauer, *Revolution and Other Writings*, 214.

126 *It is in fact our struggle*   Reclus, *Anarchy, Geography, Modernity*, 123.

128 *the example of Geronimo*   Clastres, *La société contre l'État*, 180.

130 *the monopoly of the legitimate use of physical force*   Weber, "Politics as a Vocation" (1919), in Weber, *Weber's Rationalism*, 129–98.

131 *I refuse to support any army*   Patrick Aguiar, "Déclaration de Patrick au tribunal," *Le Monde Libertaire* (online newsletter of La Fédération anarchiste, France), 3 January 1985 [Tr. JG]. http://monde-libertaire.net/?page=archives&numarchive=14737

135 *The masses remained faithful*   Préposiet, *Histoire de l'anarchie*, 108 [Tr. JG].

138 *Civil government, so far*   Smith, *Wealth of Nations*, 6th ed., vol. 2, book 5, 233.

138 *It is only under the shelter*   Ibid., 228.

138   *Without the gendarme*   Malatesta, *Anarchy*, part 7.

141   *Each individual citizen*   Sir William Beveridge, *Social Insurance and Allied Services: Report by Sir William Beveridge*, presented to the British Parliament, 26 November 1942, part VI, "Planning for Peace in War," clause 458.

143   *a mechanism designed to accumulate wealth*   Ramnath, *Decolonizing Anarchism*, 19.

144   *The amount of work given*   Kropotkin, Ibid., 249 [Tr. JG].

145   *"public services" be provided*   Marianne Enckell, "La question des services publics devant l'Internationale: fédéralisme et autonomie." *Réfractions*, no. 15 (autumn 2005), 22–23. Enckell is quoting César De Paepe.

146   *Slaves of God*   Bakunin, *God and the State* (1871), chapter 2.

153   *If God is, man is a slave*   Bakunin, Ibid., chapter 2.

153   *priests of all religions*   Bakunin, *Œuvres*, vol. 3, app. 4, 166 [Tr. JG].

155   *anarcha–indigenism*   Erica Lagalisse, "Marginalizing Magdalena: Intersections of Gender and the Secular in Anarchoindigenist Solidarity Activism," *Signs: Journal of Women in Culture and Society* 36, no. 3 (spring 2011): 653–78.

166   *I've worked in bars*   Anonymous, interviewed by Francis Dupuis-Déri, 2005 [Tr. JG].

166   *a parasitic class that feeds on the blood of others*   Michel, *Prise de possession*, 16.

166   *The origin of the wealth of the rich*   Kropotkin, *The Place of Anarchism*, 4.

166   *the domination of an individual*   Charlotte Wilson, "Social Democracy and Anarchism," *The Practical Socialist* 1, no. 1 (January 1886): 9.

167   *the dominion of man's needs*   Goldman, "Anarchism" (1910) in Goldman, *Anarchism and Other Essays*, chapter 1.

168   *We are fighting for communist anarchy*   Mühsam, *Liberating Society*, 175.

169   *The solidarity that I felt*   Thiers-Vidal, *Rupture anarchiste*, 27 [Tr. JG].

169   *the only economic science worthy*   Kropotkin, *Conquest of Bread*, chapter 4, part 3.

178   *the State having become sole proprietor*   Bakunin, *Marxism, Freedom and the State*, chapter 3.

178   *In the People's State of Marx*   Ibid., chapter 3.

180   *immense bureaucratic apparatus.*   Voline, *The Unknown Revolution*, 357.

180   *the party functionaries*   Ibid., 378.

182   *Racist theories disparage the "other."*   Sibony, *Le "Racisme,"* 16–17 [Tr. JG].

183   *Would someone be a Muslim*   Charles Boussinot, "Le patriotisme," in Faure, *L'encyclopédie anarchiste*, vol. 3 [Tr. JG].

183   *What is patriotism?*   Goldman, "What is Patriotism?" (speech 1908), in Falk and Pateman, eds. *Goldman, A Documentary History*. See also http://www.famous-speeches-and-speech-topics.info/famous-speeches/emma-goldman-speech-what-is-patriotism.htm

183   *a kind of community of ideas*   Boussinot, "Le patriotisme" [Tr. JG].

184   *As for myself, in the deeper significance*   Goldman, "A Woman Without a Country" in Patrick Weil, *The Sovereign Citizen: Denaturalization and the Origins of the American Republic* (Philadelphia: University of Pennsylvania Press, 2012), appendix 1, 195.

186   *not a white man's union*   Industrial Workers of the World, quoted in Foner, *History of the Labor Movement*, vol. 4, 125.

186   *We are 'patriotic' for our class*   Grover H. Perry, *The Revolutionary I.W.W.* (pamphlet). Chicago: I.W.W. Publishing Bureau, 1913, 7.

189   *At all times beginning with Ancient Greece*   Kropotkin, *Modern Science and Anarchism*, chapter 1.

193   *conventional methods to evaluate the effectiveness*   Amster, *Anarchism Today*.

195   *A few expected to see a revolution*   Andy Chan, "Anarchists, violence, and social change: Perspectives from today's grassroots," *Anarchist Studies* 3, no. 1 (1995): 45–68.

200   *Anarchy is order through harmony.*   Michel, quoted in Rétat, *Louise Michel* [Tr. JG].

200   *"No one owns the term 'anarchism.'"*   Chomsky, quoted in Casey, *Libertarian Anarchy*, 61.

Bibliography

Principal Works Cited

Alfred, Gerald Taiaiake. *Wasase: Indigenous Pathways of Action and Freedom*. Peterborough, Ontario: Broadview Press, 2005.

Amster, Randall. *Anarchism Today*. Santa Barbara: Praeger, 2012.

Attali, Jacques. *Demain, qui gouvernera le monde?* Paris: Fayard, 2012.

Avrich, Paul. *The Modern School Movement: Anarchism & Education in the United States*. Princeton: Princeton University Press, 2014.

Baldwin, Roger N, ed. *Kropotkin's Revolutionary Pamphlets: A Collection of Writings*. London: Dover Press, 1970.

Bakunin, Mikhail. *God and the State*. Translated by Benjamin R. Tucker. New York: Mother Earth Publishing, 1916.

———. *Marxism, Freedom and the State*. Edited and translated by K.J. Kenafick. London: Freedom Press, 1950.

———. *Œuvres*. Paris: Stock, 1895.

Bellegarrigue, Anselme. *Anarchist Manifesto*. Translated by Paul Sharkey. London: Kate Sharpley Library, 2002.

Berkman, Alexander. *Now and After: The ABC of Communist Anarchism*. New York: Vanguard Press, 1929.

Casey, Gerard. *Libertarian Anarchy Against the State*. London: Continuum, 2012.

Clastres, Pierre. *La société contre l'État*. Paris: Minuit, 1974.

Cleyre, Voltairine de. "Why I Am An Anarchist" (1897). *Mother Earth* 3 (March 1908).

Colson, Daniel. *Petit lexique anarchiste de Proudhon à Deleuze*. Paris: Librairie générale française, 2001.

215

Davis, Mike. *Les héros de l'enfer.* Paris: Textuel, 2007.

Ehrlich, Howard J., ed. *Reinventing Anarchy, Again.* Oakland: AK Press, 1996.

Eisenzweig, Uri. *Fictions de l'anarchisme.* Paris: Bourgois, 2001.

Faure, Sébastien, ed. *L'encyclopédie anarchiste.* Paris: Éditions de la Librairie internationale, 1925–34. http://www.encyclopedie-anarchiste.org/

Fernandez, Frank. *Cuban Anarchism: The History of a Movement.* Tucson, Arizona: See Sharp Press, 2001.

Feyerabend, Paul. *Against Method: Outline of an Anarchist Theory of Knowledge* (1975). New York & London: Verso, 1993.

Foner, Philip Sheldon. *History of the Labor Movement in the United States.* New York: International Publications, 1965.

Glassgold, Peter, ed. *Anarchy! An Anthology of Emma Goldman's Mother Earth.* Berkley: Counterpoint, 2001.

Goldman, Emma. *Anarchism and Other Essays.* 2nd revised edition. New York: Mother Earth Publishing, 1911.

———. *Goldman, A Documentary History of the American Years, Volume 2: Making Speech Free, 1902–1909.* Edited by Candace Falk and Barry Pateman. Champaign, IL: University of Illinois Press, 2008.

Jennings, Jeremy. *Syndicalism in France.* New York: St, Martin's Press, 1990.

Knowles, Rob. *Political Economy from Below: Economic Thought in Communitarian Anarchism, 1840–1914.* New York: Routledge, 2004.

Kropotkin, Peter. *Anarchism: A Collection of Revolutionary Writings.* New York: Dover, 2002.

———. *Anarchist Morality.* Edmonton: Black Cat Press, 2005.

———. *The Conquest of Bread.* New York and London: Putnam's Sons, 1906.

———. *Modern Science and Anarchism.* Translated by David A. Modell. Philadelphia: The Social Science Club of Philadelphia, 1903.

———. *Mutual Aid: A Factor in Evolution.* London: Heinemann, 1902.

———. *The Place of Anarchism in Socialistic Evolution.* (1884). Translated by Henry Glasse. London: International Publishing Company, n.d. www.theanarchistlibrary.org

———. *La science moderne et l'anarchie.* Revised and enlarged 1913 French edition of *Modern Science and Anarchism.* Villiers-sur Marne: Phénix éditions, 2004.

———. *The State: Its Historic Role.* Translated by Vernon Richards. London: Free Press, 1946.

———. *Words of a Rebel: Origins and Developments.* Translated by George Woodcock. Montreal: Black Rose Books, 1992.

Landauer, Gustave. *Revolution and Other Writings: A Political Reader.* Edited and translated by Gabriel Kuhn. Oakland: PM Press, 2010.

Leier, Mark. *Bakunin: The Creative Passion: A Biography.* New York: Thomas Dunne Books/St. Martin's Press, 2006.

Loye, David. *Darwin's Lost Theory: Bridge to a Better World.* Carmel, CA: The Benjamin Franklin Press, 2007.

Malatesta, Errico. *Anarchy.* Translated by Vernon Richards. London: Freedom Press, 1974.

Marechal, Sylvain. *Manifesto of the Equals.* In Philippe Buonarroti, *La conspiration pour l'égalité* (1830). Paris: Editions Sociales, 1957. Translated by Mitchell Abidor for marxist.org

Maximoff, G.P., ed. *The Political Philosophy of Bakunin: Scientific Anarchism.* London: The Free Press of Glencoe, 1953.

Mbah, Sam, and I.E. Igariwey. *African Anarchism: The History of a Movement.* Tucson, Arizona: See Sharp Press, 1977.

Michel, Louise. *Prise de possession.* Paris: Éditions d'Ores et déjà, 2009.

Mühsam, Erich. *Liberating Society from the State, And Other Writings: A Political Reader.* Edited and translated by Gabriel Kuhn. Oakland: PM Press, 2011.

Préposiet, Jean. *Histoire de l'anarchisme.* Paris: Pluriel, 2012.

Proudhon, Pierre Joseph. *What is Property? An Inquiry Into the Principle of Right and of Government* (1840). Translated by Benjamin R. Tucker. New York: Humboldt, 1890. marxists.org.

Ramnath, Maia. *Decolonizing Anarchism: An Antiauthoritarian History of India's Liberation Struggle.* Chico, Calif.: AK Press, 2011.

Reclus, Élisée. "L'anarchie" (1894). Paris: Éditions du Sextant, 2006.
———. *Anarchy, Geography, Modernity: Selected Writings of Elisée Reclus.* Edited by John P. Clark and Camille Martin. Oakland: PM Press, 2013.
———. *L'évolution, la révolution et l'idéal anarchique* (1898). Paris: Éditions Phénix, 2001.

Rétat, Claude. ed., *Louise Michel: À travers la mort: Mémoires inédits, 1886–1890.* Paris: La Découverte, 2002.

Sahlins, Marshall. *The Western Illusion of Human Nature.* Chicago: Prickly Paradigm Press, 2008.

Sibony, Daniel. *Le "Racisme," une haine identitaire.* Paris: Christian Bourgois, 1997.

Smith, Adam. *An Inquiry Into the Nature and Causes of the Wealth of Nations.* 6th ed. London: George Bell & Sons, 1887.

Thiers-Vidal, Léo. *Rupture anarchiste et trahison pro-féministe.* Lyon: Éditions Bambule, 2013.

Voline. *The Unknown Revolution, 1917–1921.* Translated by Holley

Cantine and Fredy Perlman. Montreal: Black Rose Books, 1990.
Weber, Max. *Weber's Rationalism and Modern Society: New Transla-
tions on Politics, Bureaucracy, and Social Stratification.* Translated and
edited by Tony Waters and Dagmar Waters. New York: Palgrave
Macmillan, 2015.

Suggested Further Readings

Dark Star Collective, ed. *Quiet Rumors: An Anarcha-Feminist Reader.*
Chico, Calif.: AK Press, 2012.
Gay, Kathlyn, and Martin K. Gay. *Encyclopedia of Political Anarchy.*
Santa Barbara: ABC-Clio, 1999.
Gordon, Uri. *Anarchy Alive!: Anti-Authoritarian Politics from Practice to
Theory.* London: Pluto Press, 2008.
Graham, Robert, ed. *Anarchism: A Documentary History of Libertarian
Ideas.* 3 vols. Montreal: Black Rose Books, 2004.
Kinna, Ruth. *Anarchism: A Beginner's Guide.* London: Oneworld Pub-
lications, 2005.
McKay, Iain, ed. *An Anarchist FAQ.* 2 vols. Chico, Calif: AK Press,
2012.
Milstein, Cindy. *Anarchism and Its Aspirations.* Chico, Calif: AK Press,
2010.
Shantz, Jeff. *Active Anarchy: Political Practice in Contemporary Move-
ments.* Lanham, MD: Lexington Books, 2011.
Woodcock, George. *Anarchism: A History of Libertarian Ideas and
Movements.* New York: Meridian Book, 1962.

Works by Francis Dupuis-Déri in English

BOOKS
Who's Afraid of the Black Blocs? Anarchy in Action Around the World.
Translated by Lazer Lederhendler. Oakland: PM Press, 2014.

ARTICLES
"The Political Power of Words: The Birth of Pro-Democratic Dis-
course in the 19th Century in the United States and France." *Political Studies* 52 (2004): 118–34.
"Anarchy in Political Philosophy." *Anarchist Studies* 13, no.1 (2005):
9–23.
"Global protesters versus global elites: Are direct action and deliber-
ative politics compatible?" *New Political Science* 29, no. 2 (2007):
167–86.
"What about patriarchy? Some thoughts of a heterosexual anarcho-
male." *Social Anarchism* 43 (2009): 60–80.

"Anarchism and the politics of affinity groups." *Anarchist Studies* 18, no. 1 (2010): 40–61.

"History of the word 'democracy' in Canada and Quebec: A political analysis of rhetorical strategies." *World Political Science Review* 6, no. 2 (2010): 1–23.

"The Black Blocs ten years after Seattle." *Journal for the Study of Radicalism* 4, no.2 (2010): 45–82.

"Anarchism and human nature: Domination vs. autonomy." *Social Anarchism*, no 45 (2012): 41–52.

"Herbert Marcuse and the 'Antiglobalization' movement: Thinking through radical opposition to neoliberal globalization." *Radical Philosophy Review* 16, no. 2 (2013): 529–47.

"Is the State part of the matrix of domination and intersectionality? An anarchist inquiry."*Anarchist Studies* 4, no. 1 (2016): 36–61.